SITE
COMMUNITY
ICON
INNOVATION

THE ARCHITECTURE
OF SMITHGROUP

**ESSAYS BY
ANNE GUINEY**

First published in the
United States of America by
Edizioni Press, Inc.
469 West 21st Street
New York, New York 10011
www.edizionipress.com

ISBN: 1-931536-37-6
Library of Congress Catalogue
Card Number: 2004093372

Design: Project Projects
Editor: Aaron Seward
Editorial Assistant: Sarah Palmer
Printed in China

FOREWORD

by Bruce Alberts PhD,
President, National Academy of Sciences

Although an eager scientist-in-training with almost no prior interest in the subject, someone convinced me to take Harvard College's two-semester, introductory art and architecture course (Fine Arts 13) for credit shortly before I graduated. Nearly everything that I would learn in this survey course would be new to me, and this was especially true for the section on architecture.

As one particularly memorable assignment, we were asked to study and write papers about several of Harvard's elegant buildings—both in Harvard Yard and at the law school. Ever since that experience, I have looked at our human-built world with completely different eyes. The same building exteriors that I had ignored during my early years at Harvard are now objects of art that give me great pleasure to analyze, and I now take the time to stop and gaze. In the same vein, each visit to Paris or London provides an opportunity to spend at least a little time carefully comparing the façades on randomly selected blocks of old apartments. Why, I wonder, are the complex forms of some objects pleasing to humans, while others are distasteful? This is a deep question, and for a scientist like myself the answers we seek are presently out of reach due to our inadequate understandings of the molecular, cellular, and network basis for the pleasure centers in the human brain.

All of us who live in the modern world are deeply affected by architects and architecture, even if we know nothing at all about the subject. Much more than we would like to admit, architects have profoundly shaped our lives through the ways that they have designed homes, the buildings where we work, and—on a larger scale—our urban and suburban landscapes. The landscapes that they create can either inspire or alienate the human spirit. In my neighborhood, I always find a walk in Georgetown invigorating, whereas taking a similar walk just across the Potomac River in Rosslyn, Virginia is a dehumanizing experience. It is the urban planners and the architects who have created this difference, and it is one that is likely to persist for hundreds of years. An architect bears a great burden as she or he creates a new design; more than almost any other profession, what emerges is likely to have a profound effect on the lives of large numbers of people, including many not yet born.

It is of course not only the exteriors of buildings that matter; the design of building interiors are often even more critical in profoundly affecting the way that people live and work together. Before moving to my full-time position at the National Academy of Sciences in 1993, I spent 30 years as a research scientist—at Harvard, Princeton, and, finally, at the University of California, San Francisco (UCSF). It quickly became clear to me that science flourishes only in certain physical environments, being particularly sensitive to the way that the different groups of laboratories in each institution are arranged in relationship to each other. Why?

The answer depends on recognizing that science is very much a community activity, in which new knowledge is built upon combinations of old knowledge in novel, unpredictable ways. Contrary to a popular misconception, the best science is almost never done by an isolated genius locked away in his or her laboratory. Instead, a productive research environment requires a laboratory arrangement that causes the frequent random collisions of scientists who have different knowledge and ideas. Show me a department of molecular biology (my field of science) that occupies a research building in which each laboratory serves as its own separate island—so that the scientists in different laboratories need to pass each other only twice a day (arriving in the morning and leaving at night)—and I will show you a research environment that deadens scientific productivity. The architects who designed that building have made it very difficult for good science to flourish no matter how beautiful the structure.

By chance, I presently occupy two of the buildings that are described in this beautiful book of architectural examples. I was intimately involved in the planning and design of the new National Academy of Sciences building at 500 5th Street in Washington, DC, where I presently work (see p. 56). In addition, I have recently been given a new office 2500 miles away at the University of California, San Francisco, Mission Bay Genentech Hall (see p. 174).

Despite the very different types of activities that they house, the designs of these two buildings are related in spirit and intention. The laboratory designs in Genentech Hall were based on those that had been refined earlier in a continuous improvement cycle, moving from floor to floor in the two research towers at UCSF's main campus on Parnassus Avenue. Based on the input of the scientists who worked in them, they had been optimized to create a highly interactive environment, where the faculty and students from different laboratories are constantly colliding to exchange their ideas and their dreams. When we began to work in Washington on our new building, one of the prime challenges for the architects was to design an interior that would similarly force the nearly 1000-person staff of the National Academies to interact, both on their office floors and in the large atrium that forms the "town center" for community life—with its cafeteria, library, credit union, and professional development center.

Like Genentech Hall, the new building of the National Academy of Sciences is viewed as a major success, fulfilling its promise as a stimulating environment for producing the best possible work in science policy. It has already done a great deal to move the physicists, biologists, engineers, social scientists, and medical experts out of the intellectual silos that each had tended to develop in their previous locations. It is a building that explicitly builds a work community—thereby helping us to better serve the nation by bringing the widest possible mix of relevant expertise to bear on each of the many important studies that we are asked to carry out for the government.

1

RESPONDING TO SITE: NECESSITY AND INSPIRATION

SmithGroup's nine offices—Ann Arbor, Chicago, Detroit, Los Angeles, Madison, Minneapolis, Phoenix, San Francisco, and Washington, DC—work around the country in contexts as varied and complex as the country itself. To work well in such a broad field, and to respond to the peculiarities of each site, the firm has organized itself more along the model of a federation than a standard corporation. The nine offices have design autonomy, and so there is a plurality of styles and approaches in the work coming out of each. They do not work in isolation, of course—there are national design reviews several times a year, but these focus less on the aesthetic of the project in development than on its internal logic, and whether or not that logic can be clarified. The resulting eclecticism is not a sign of divergent interests in the different offices, but of a firm-wide commitment to regionalism, and an ability to thoroughly digest the culture of each region and each client.

At first, it might be hard to see the family resemblance between the dark and monolithic form of the Arizona Western College Career Center, to the elegant vernacular of the shed-like building at Indian Springs Metropark Environmental Education Center in Michigan, but they are there. Their kinship lies in the way that each manifests a local understanding of the peculiarities of a given landscape overlaid on the respective building's program. (This approach is one in which micro, mid, and macro scales must come into play. Site analysis must also consider a range of issues from topographic irregularities to a historic neighborhood with a strict formal review process, to a strip-mall-like lack of any coherency, and even to the demographics of the user groups. That last concern, while not typically one of site, is important because it will shape a building's gestures to its users, who in turn can change the building's personality.)

The Arizona Western College (AWC) Career Center is an interesting example of how one might understand SmithGroup's process. While the immediate physical site is not spectacular— it sits at a highway's edge six miles from the main campus— the grand profile of Chocolate Mountain is always visible in the distance. The community of users, too, is not always the same as those at AWC's main campus—the focus here is on job training and placement. English as a Second Language, General Equivalency Degree classes, and Senior Learning are some of the offerings, and each costs a modest 36 dollars per credit hour. Recent immigrants and skiers—two groups one might not think have a lot in common besides mobility—are the main consumers of the career center's opportunities.

In form, the career center shows the influence of the work of an emerging regional school in Arizona, whose practitioners have developed a vocabulary heavily inspired by the extraordinary nature of the landscape, with elements that reference both that landscape and its history. Monumental forms reference the pre-modern buildings of the Native American tribes who once lived there, the architecture of Spanish Colonialists who began to displace them, and the unforgiving climate that their buildings exploited. Thus for the career center, the site is not just the interstate nearby, but the mountain in the distance whose coloration it echoes, and the harsh sun whose strength it defies. In symbolic terms, its bold form gives a quality of permanence and commitment that quietly underscores the center's educational philosophy of accessibility for all. Taking a class or using the computer room may be the first step toward further learning for many of its users, and the building has more than enough ceremony to applaud that decision.

Indian Springs Metropark Environmental Education Center in Michigan has a similarly attentive attitude toward its site, which is an enormous wetlands preserve outside of Detroit. Here, though, the defiant stance taken at the career center wouldn't make any sense physically or aesthetically, so Indian Springs adopts a more delicate posture. As if to shelter the fragile ecology of the area from the impingements of the automobile, the building presents a solid face toward the parking lot from which people enter: the copper roof folds down over the limestone wall like an insect's exoskeleton, a tough shell that protects a tender body. The opposite side, however, is entirely open: a glazed façade and colonnade embrace the marsh, so that, once inside the building, visitors are in an entirely different landscape. The building's seemingly dual nature gives a quiet signal to curious Detroiters that the world they come from—that of the automobile—can be temporarily left behind, and that this new world can be explored in contemplative detail.

The Indian Springs facility's foremost purpose is education; it is animated by the hope that greater awareness of the Huron Swamp will inspire the general public to better protect it. Along with classrooms and several environmental laboratories, the building has an observation room submerged in a plexiglass bubble under the water's surface, so one can see the pond's rich life at close hand without causing it any harm. Like the Arizona Western College Career Center, its attitude of deference toward the land and visitors points to an understanding of site that goes beyond logistics and constraints to a respect born of understanding. That this deferential attitude toward site can take such dramatically different forms in two buildings by the same firm is testament to the sensibility that unites the SmithGroup architects.

U.S. FISH AND WILDLIFE SERVICE
NATIONAL CONSERVATION TRAINING CENTER
SHEPHERDSTOWN, WEST VIRGINIA 1997

The U.S. Fish and Wildlife Service (USFWS) works to conserve, protect, and enhance fish, wildlife, and plants and their habitats for the continued benefit of the American people. Education is a central part of the USFWS mission, so it commissioned SmithGroup to design a campus facility to create a base for educating its own staffers and members of the interested public on the latest science and best management practices for wildlife biology. In fulfilling the USFWS vision of creating a home for the service, the new 365,000-square-foot, 14-building National Conservation Training Center features an administration/main auditorium/museum building; instructional buildings with training space and offices for the training staff, seminar/classrooms, and offices; and laboratory buildings with biomedical and freshwater teaching laboratories. The residential campus features three 50-unit dormitories. The "social" campus has a commons lodge with a dining room, cafeteria, lounge, and library, and a physical training building. The environmental education campus, where teachers learn how to discuss environmental issues, features the education programs office building, training and education material production building, including audio and TV studios and library, and a daycare center. It is a comprehensive educational

environment supporting almost 10,000 visiting students a year and a full-time staff of 200. In addition, the center has also been used by government and business groups as a retreat/conference center.

As a way of extending the facility's educational aspects, both SmithGroup and the USFWS realized that the relationship between the center and the land in which it sits should be as harmonious as possible. The architects set the campus core deep within the 500-acre site, resting the buildings below knolls and behind trees, so that the campus is obscured from the site's perimeter. Low building heights and modest footprints further minimize the installation's impact on the terrain. The area's history, farmland, and natural resources provide content for an interpretive trail system and outdoor training.

The design of the buildings is based on a contemporary interpretation of the local vernacular of mid-Atlantic farm and mill structures and also uses the 18th-century farm buildings still extant on the property as a "pattern." The use of local masonry, 75% recycled steel siding, engineered wood products, and natural and durable interior finishes with minimal off-gassing properties assured that the structures would not only respect their context, but also rest lightly on the land.

PREVIOUS: The architecture of the center seeks a
harmonious relationship with the land.
ABOVE: The buildings rest in the center of the
500-acre site. DRAWING: Site plan

ABOVE: Building materials include local masonry,
recycled steel siding, and engineered wood products.
BELOW: The residential campus

ABOVE: The use of natural materials is evident throughout the interiors.

ARIZONA WESTERN COLLEGE CAREER CENTER
YUMA, ARIZONA 1999

Located in the Sonoran desert, Yuma possesses a culturally diverse past. Long inhabited by the Quechan and Cocopah Indians, and visited by the Spaniards in 1540, the town's formation was most influenced by the mining booms and the arrival of the railroad. The damming of the Colorado River in the early 1900s made irrigation possible, and transformed the fertile desert valley into rich farmland and citrus groves.

In an effort to provide community education for the area, Arizona Western College commissioned the Phoenix office of SmithGroup to design the 22,000-square-foot career center. Situated on a five-acre site on the eastern edge of town six miles from the main campus, the facility's primary purpose is to provide access to continuing education and professional development. The programmatic focus is on classrooms, computer labs, and administrative support for outreach programs.

SmithGroup took aesthetic cues from the historical Territorial Style typical of the region, hence the mass of the structure, punched openings, shaded courtyard, and covered walkways. The colors of the exterior concrete masonry walls are also in character with the landscape: purple and chocolate-colored elements are contrasted with desert tans. Silver/gray Galvalum screen walls reflect the abundance of agricultural buildings and the Airstream trailers so popular in the area.

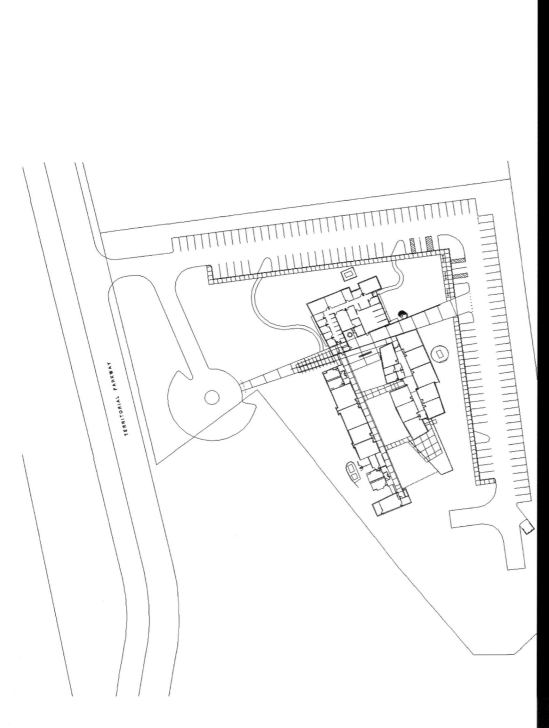

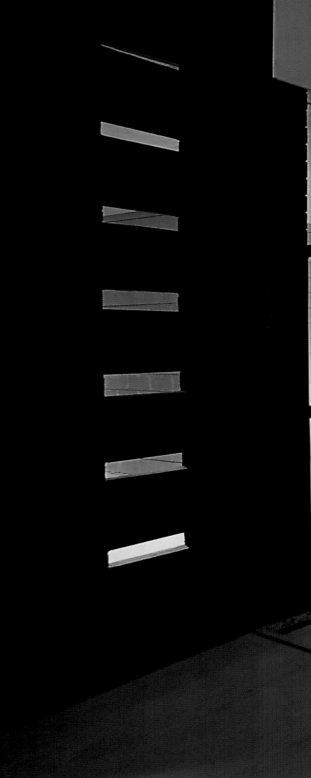

PREVIOUS: The architecture takes its cues from
the historical Territorial Style of the region.
ABOVE, LEFT TO RIGHT: Silver, purple, red, and desert
tans make up the color palette. DRAWING: Site plan

ABOVE: The student-focused courtyard

JACKSON NATIONAL LIFE INSURANCE COMPANY, CORPORATE HEADQUARTERS
LANSING, MICHIGAN 2000

Jackson National Life Insurance Company is one of the country's largest and strongest financial services companies. SmithGroup designed their 317,500-square-foot corporate headquarters on a previously undeveloped parcel of land adjacent to a 200-acre wooded site. Aside from providing both open and closed workstations for the 1,200 employees, the building features conference areas, a fitness center, and a food court-styled dining area with indoor and outdoor seating for 300 employees. A corporate sponsored daycare center is a crucial part of the campus, allowing employees to interact with their children at lunch hours.

To take advantage of the beauty of the surrounding woods, SmithGroup created a four-story facility that is long and narrow in plan. Every work area in the building is thus open to the wooded surrounds, and streaming daylight penetrates deep into the floor-plate. The entry façade forms the concave side of an arch, which embraces visitors and employees approaching from the parking lots. The stone and galvanized metal here relate to the nearby farmsteads of rural Lansing. At the rear elevation, a convex shape is formed entirely of cantilevered glass.

A continuous public circulation path allows each employee a panoramic view of the woodland and stream beyond. To encourage vertical movement and interaction between employees, SmithGroup incorporated four monumental stairs at intervals along the building.

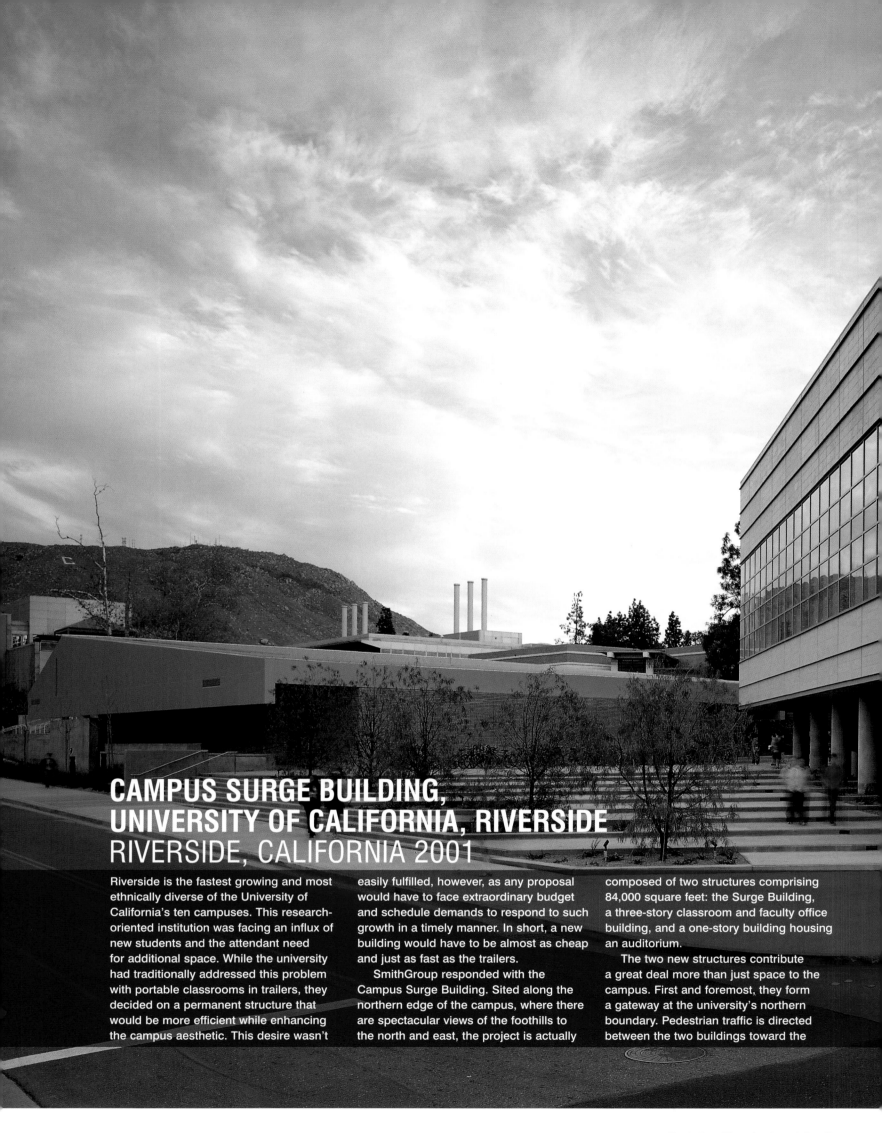

CAMPUS SURGE BUILDING, UNIVERSITY OF CALIFORNIA, RIVERSIDE
RIVERSIDE, CALIFORNIA 2001

Riverside is the fastest growing and most ethnically diverse of the University of California's ten campuses. This research-oriented institution was facing an influx of new students and the attendant need for additional space. While the university had traditionally addressed this problem with portable classrooms in trailers, they decided on a permanent structure that would be more efficient while enhancing the campus aesthetic. This desire wasn't

easily fulfilled, however, as any proposal would have to face extraordinary budget and schedule demands to respond to such growth in a timely manner. In short, a new building would have to be almost as cheap and just as fast as the trailers.

SmithGroup responded with the Campus Surge Building. Sited along the northern edge of the campus, where there are spectacular views of the foothills to the north and east, the project is actually

composed of two structures comprising 84,000 square feet: the Surge Building, a three-story classroom and faculty office building, and a one-story building housing an auditorium.

The two new structures contribute a great deal more than just space to the campus. First and foremost, they form a gateway at the university's northern boundary. Pedestrian traffic is directed between the two buildings toward the

ABOVE: The simple repetitive system of ceramic tiles with aluminum reveals and brick allowed for a substantial but low-cost façade.

core of the campus. The circulation path also connects this part of the campus with nearby student housing.

The challenge for SmithGroup was to develop substantial looking buildings that interacted well with the rest of the campus' sturdy materials of brick, cast-in-place concrete, and metal panels for the same price as far less substantial exterior plaster. In response to these budget constraints, the façade of the Surge Building is a simple system of repetitive elements. At the ground level, a buff-colored brick relates to the campus' dominant building material. A taut skin of ceramic tiles, accented with aluminum reveals, clads the second and third floors.

The Surge Building and Auditorium are composed as background and fore-ground objects, respectively. Due to its size and repetitive nature, the Surge Building recedes behind the Auditorium, which operates as a sculptural figure due to its sectional development and sloped roof profile. Inside, the Auditorium simulates an acoustically live space with the state-of-the-art audio/visual systems that encourage student/teacher interaction. Its dramatic ceiling is reflected on the exterior by the roof form, which has become a permanent landmark for the campus, visible to both vehicles and pedestrians.

BOVARD AUDITORIUM, UNIVERSITY OF SOUTHERN CALIFORNIA
LOS ANGELES, CALIFORNIA 2003

University of Southern California's historic Bovard Auditorium rests at the heart of the University Park campus. It serves as a venue for a wide variety of events, including musical and theatrical performances, and campus convocations. In addition to needing various entertainment-oriented improvements, such as a functioning lobby, the 1920s building had to be brought up to current codes. SmithGroup renovated 26,000 square feet of the existing auditorium and added another 1,747 square feet of new lobby space at the first balcony level. The project was fast-tracked, and was designed and constructed in just ten months.

SmithGroup used a series of graceful contemporary interventions to enhance and complement the neo-gothic shell, attempting to find a balance between the restoration of the existing historic structure and the introduction of a series of architectural elements that express the present. The architects worked with acoustical consultants Kirkegaard & Associates to improve the auditorium's acoustics and with Auerback-Pollock-Friedlander, a theatrical consultant, to redesign the theatrical systems. These changes give the facility greater flexibility as a multipurpose performance venue. They redesigned the seating layout and stage design to increase comfort and improve sightlines, and the new lobby space allows for a single point of entry for all visitors versus the existing six separate entries. Historical consultant Kaplan, Chen & Kaplan were hired to maintain the existing details, including portions of the main entry and aspects of the large windows.

PREVIOUS: The redesigned seating layout and stage improve sight lines and comfort. FACING PAGE: View of the Julliard Quartet performing from the second balcony DRAWING: Ground floor plan RIGHT: Front lobby LEFT: A stair in the side lobby

ESTRELLA MOUNTAIN COMMUNITY COLLEGE, KOMATKE HALL
AVONDALE, ARIZONA 2003

Estrella Mountain Community College is a component of the Maricopa County Community College District, the largest community college district in the country. It sits at the western edge of the Phoenix metropolitan area, where urban sprawl gives way to the desert environment. The renovation and expansion of Komatke Hall was very much influenced by this context; both conceptually and program-matically, SmithGroup imagined the project as a modern-day desert oasis.

While a portion of the existing 17,120-square-foot hall structure was renovated to house administrative offices, a connecting new building was constructed just to the west. The new building provides space for one-stop student enrollment services and

administrative support, as well as areas for food services, student activities, and the kitchen and classroom of the culinary arts program. In plan, each of these elements is arranged around an interior campus courtyard, which, with its fountain, is a true respite from the desert's heat. Together the existing and new structures comprise 47,586 square feet and combine the needs of the college's student and staff services into one cohesive complex.

The building exterior is designed to react harmoniously with the Sonoran desert environment. The cast-in-place concrete walls have a warm earth-toned color and the concrete masonry units were stained to match the existing campus palette. A trellis-covered passage that

leads between the two new buildings from the south parking lot to the courtyard is lined entirely by floor-to-ceiling glazing. Just inside, built-in art displays feature student and traveling art shows, thus creating an inviting entry procession for visitors and students.

The design of the interior had to create a flexible environment capable of handling rapid changes in technology and the swiftly expanding population of the area. The school chose the flexibility of systems furniture, due to its ability to be reconfigured as the need arises, and added a new technically adaptable system for the self-enrollment computer area.

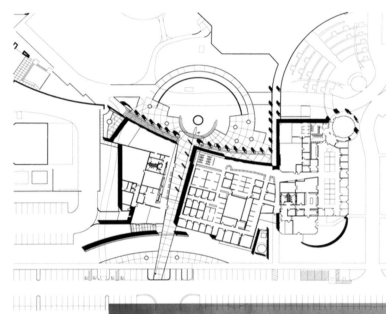

PREVIOUS: Artist Barbara Grygutis designed the entrance canopy's sculptural column covers. **DRAWING:** Floor plan **ABOVE:** The courtyard at night **BELOW LEFT:** A hole in the patio wall offers a view of the Estrella Mountains. **BELOW RIGHT:** Indigenous plants in the courtyard **FACING PAGE:** Shading casts light patterns along the pedestrian arcade.

INDIAN SPRINGS METROPARK, ENVIRONMENTAL EDUCATION CENTER
OAKLAND COUNTY, MICHIGAN 2004

The Huron-Clinton Metropolitan Authority, "Metroparks," is a regional special park district that provides an ever-growing variety of outdoor recreational and educational activities the year round in safe, clean environments. The authority is particularly dedicated to environmental education and preservation. Indian Springs Metropark is one of 13 such sites located along the Huron and Clinton rivers that form a greenbelt around the Detroit metropolitan area. It sits at the headwaters of the Huron River, which are known as Huron Swamp. The 70-acre site comprises a mix of wetlands and gently rolling hills covered with brush vegetation and some mature woods.

Metropark's administration needed a facility to introduce schoolchildren and the general public to the nature and benefits of wetlands, and they called on SmithGroup to design the Environmental Education Center. The program called for a multipurpose room accommodating 280 people seated at tables, a wet environmental laboratory for 30 students, and two environmental dry classrooms for typical grade school classes. An underwater immersion classroom, administrative areas, and provisions for a future distance education room were also needed.

The center takes its cues from the low rolling hills of the Metropark, which are just high enough to hide the building from view until crested or passed. The roof folds over, creating a gently sloping edge of copper roofing that meets the wall's limestone ledge-rock and hides the wetland from the view of the parking lot. Visitors enter the three-story, 18,000-square-foot building at the top, or ground floor, and then descend one flight to the pond level. Here, an open colonnade along the water's edge allows them a protected view of the extraordinary, if quiet landscape. For most of the younger visitors, the real thrill will be the underwater immersion classroom, which is the building's lowest level. This 20-foot in diameter, clear acrylic room enables visitors to explore the wetlands from below the waterline and engage the complexities of the ecosystem face to face.

ABOVE: South façade of the center as seen from across the pond

LA KRETZ HALL,
UNIVERSITY OF CALIFORNIA, LOS ANGELES
LOS ANGELES, CALIFORNIA 2004

The 20,000-square-foot La Kretz Hall is positioned at a critical pedestrian node at UCLA—the south end of the court of sciences—and will serve as conferencing and classroom space to many of the adjacent research laboratories. The program called for two basic components: classrooms, including a 350-seat auditorium and a 45-seat distance learning room for the Undergraduate College of Letters and Sciences; and offices for the Institute of the Environment, a group of scientists, engineers, and architects conducting joint research on environmental conditions in the Los Angeles Basin.

The real challenge for SmithGroup was that the building is actually sited atop the concrete roof slab of a five-million-gallon chilled water storage tank. Although the tank was designed to carry the weight of the new building, the specifics of attaching the structures required several innovative structural solutions to integrate the two. These included methods of connection between building and tank, planning of the spaces on the ground floor, and hybrid seismic solutions, which use both moment and eccentrically braced framing systems.

The result is a building that is a product of its environment both geometrically and aesthetically. Its materials—UCLA blend Norman brick and terracotta-colored elements—respond to the character of the university's Romanesque campus core, while the plan is a product of the geometry of the tank itself, specifically as it inflects to accept a grand stair. A third floor is free from the geometrical restraints below and is a lightweight glass and steel pavilion of offices.

SmithGroup and UCLA planned La Kretz Hall to be a LEED™-certified (Leadership in Energy and Environmental Design) sustainable design project. An under floor displacement air supply system ventilates the auditorium, while high and low operable windows in the offices upstairs take advantage of the mild climate.

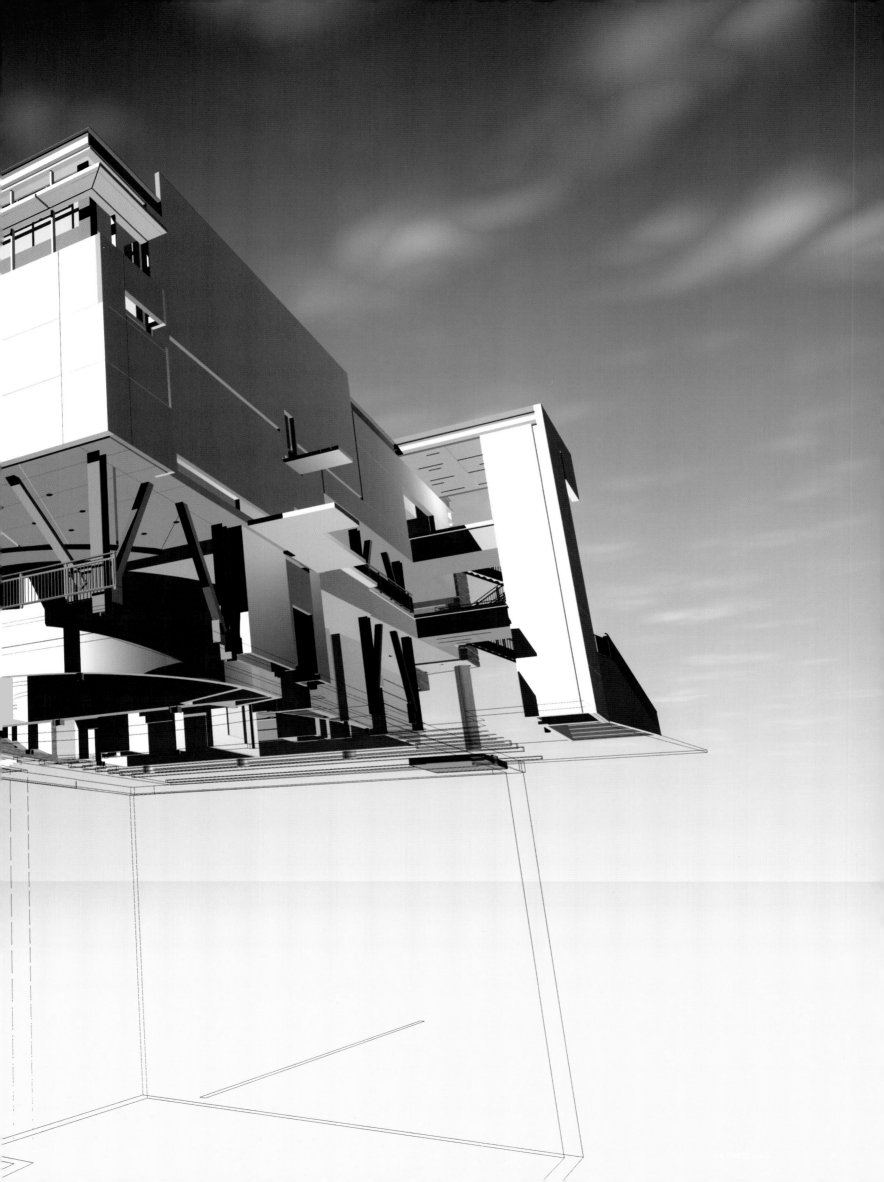

PREVIOUS: Southwest view of La Kretz Hall showing the
water tank in outline ABOVE: The auditorium
BELOW: The building is entered via a grand stair.

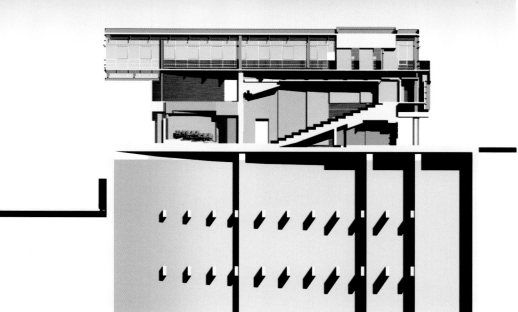

U.S. ARID-LAND AGRICULTURAL RESEARCH CENTER
MARICOPA, ARIZONA 2005

The U.S. Arid-Land Agricultural Research Center conducts research on environmental stewardship and water conservation for the agricultural industry in the Southwest. Strategically sited adjacent to the University of Arizona's agricultural research farm, 25 miles south of Phoenix, the center's offices, labs, lab support spaces, greenhouses, outbuildings, and agricultural research plots are integrated into an existing campus plan.

SmithGroup arranged the 100,000 square feet of programmatically disparate components as a collection of low-rise elements that formally represent their functions. The architects found inspiration for the center in the indigenous farm and ranch buildings found throughout Arizona. These native structures exploit the possibilities of orientation, locally manufactured materials, and serene, environmentally protective exterior courtyard spaces; their enduring presence points the way to a locally appropriate and sustainable architecture.

The entire site is woven together with covered metal deck walkways. Functional vertical elements, such as the grove of trees in the courtyard and the laboratory exhaust stacks, provide visual relief to the horizontal composition of earth-toned concrete walls. Corrugated galvanized steel roofs acoustically herald the occasional storm and demonstrate environmentally responsible water harvesting by collecting rainfall into a cistern, which will then flow, via gravity, to irrigation canals in the courtyard.

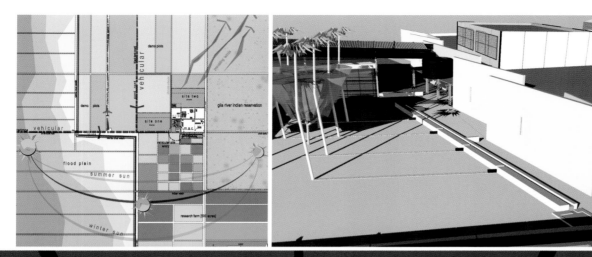

PREVIOUS: The entrance canopy functions as both a shading and water collection device.
DRAWING: Site plan ABOVE: The courtyard
BELOW: A shaded pedestrian promenade

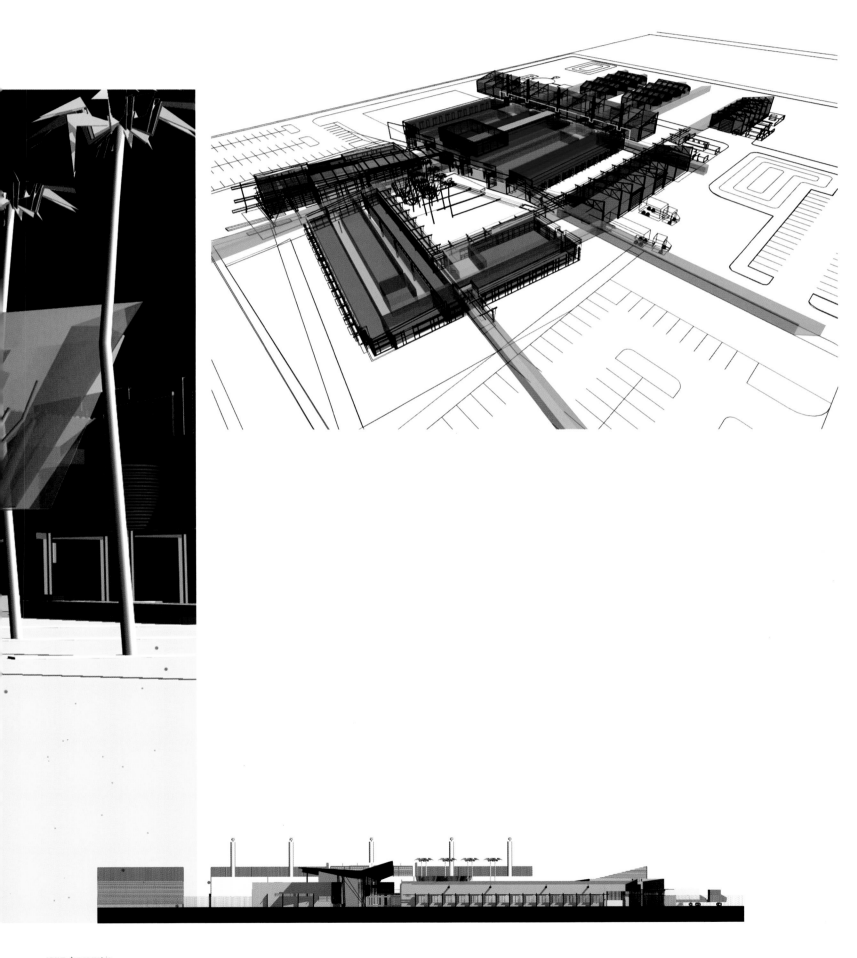

2

BUILDING COMMUNITY, COMMUNITY BUILDINGS

Community is often an idea as much as it is a geographical reality. One of the extraordinary things about life in a city is the way that thousands of groups—brought together by interest, physical neighborhood, ethnicity, age, and profession—overlay one another, interlocking at some points and not at others as if in some massive Venn diagram. Communities take shape when groups of people rally around a certain trait or set of values and come together when that self-definition is challenged. As a whole, the architectural profession has a fairly mixed record in the community-building department, but this is testament to the difficulty in defining what that community is and deciding what a building must do.

SmithGroup's body of work may help improve the profession's average, because of its underlying belief in looking first at what each community's constituent parts are, or what with help they can be. At Indiana University Purdue University Indianapolis (IUPUI), the problem is fairly straightforward, if not necessarily easy to solve: provide a physical and emotional center to support IUPUI's transition from a predominantly commuter environment to a traditional pedestrian university environment. The new campus center has an accordingly clear but nuanced attitude. The program includes everything from lounges, a gallery, copy facilities, to a food court, all arranged around a large glazed atrium with a tall campanile. (It is no stretch to imagine the place packed with students throughout the day, reading, gossiping, or debating the issues of the day.) The project goes one step further by giving the center a grand symbolic face. The bell tower creates a visible and audible reference point for the students and faculty moving around campus, and it connects the building to an old and venerable tradition in campus buildings.

Another campus project presents a thornier and more contemporary problem, which the architects have resolved in a successfully contemporary way. In program, the multipurpose building at the University of California, San Diego, is essentially a temporary shelter for various academic departments waiting for a permanent home, and it actually replaces the trailers that once served this purpose. Departments constantly cycling in and out precluded having spaces specific to any one discipline. The multipurpose building approaches the problem by looking outward and making subtle contributions to the larger public realm, so that, while its inhabitants ultimately make the decisions as to how they choose to interact, the many public spaces and points of visual connection provide the opportunity for community to form.

SmithGroup's many years of community-building work in many places have convinced them of at least this one thing: in most cases, communities are not made by fiat. It often happens that the design process itself can strengthen the bonds of community as much as the resulting building. By asking a client to think long and hard about competing obligations to the building's future users, any divisions within the group will be laid bare. In asking how a group of people defines itself and its needs, one helps a consensus to grow. And if the complexity of the group's answers leads to a more complex spatial experience, then a good foundation is in place, because a building must ultimately evolve along with its community's understanding of itself.

UNIVERSITY OF ARIZONA SARVER HEART CENTER
TUCSON, ARIZONA 2000

Located at the medical center of the University of Arizona campus, the new 35,000-square-foot Sarver Heart Center was built on top of the existing college of medicine and adjacent to the basic sciences wing of the Arizona Health Sciences Center. The new three-level facility allows the heart center to expand its research efforts, which are focused on searching for cures for heart and vascular diseases, and responds to the increasing need for preventative education. The program includes offices for the heart center's administration, space for outreach programs and preventative education, wet and dry laboratory modules, computer labs, research offices, and laboratory support facilities.

Though it is perched atop an existing building, the Sarver Heart Center is integrated within the university community by a private entrance on the ground floor, designed by SmithGroup to invite patients, their families, and the general public to access information and participate in clinical research. The entry sequence begins at curbside, where a walkway guides visitors to a glass elevator and up to the reception area on the fourth floor, which is the first of the center's three levels.

The overall massing of the Sarver Heart Center features emerging forms that articulate the major building elevations. The challenge for this design was to create a public outreach facility with a unique personality, one that is different from its 1960s Modern-style base and neighboring facilities.

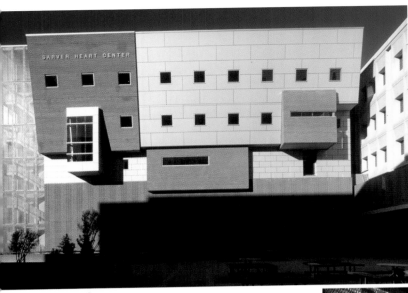

PREVIOUS: Metal panels form a gasket between the existing and new construction. **ABOVE LEFT:** Program requirements animate the building envelope. **ABOVE RIGHT AND BELOW:** A glass elevator and stair tower lead visitors to the fourth floor reception area. **FACING PAGE:** The addition's character is distinct from the 1960s modernist base.

UNIVERSITY OF ARIZONA SARVER HEART CENTER 49

MOTION PICTURE & TELEVISION FUND, FRAN & RAY STARK ASSISTED LIVING VILLA
WOODLAND HILLS, CALIFORNIA 2001

The Motion Picture & Television Fund is dedicated to serving members of the entertainment industry. Its efforts go far beyond traditional healthcare, offering a continuum of services that range from quality medical and surgical services, childcare, residential living, and care for older adults, as well as social and charitable services. Located on the undeveloped half of the fund's 46-acre Wasserman Campus, which was built in 1944 and includes a hospital, Alzheimer's care facility, outpatient health village, and additional assisted-living, The Fran & Ray Stark Assisted Living Villa offers housing for up to 90 residents.

The villa's architects looked beyond the stereotypes of senior housing to reflect a modern attitude that fosters community, social interaction, dignity, and independence. Arriving at the villa, one enters through the main living room. From there, single-loaded corridors, leading to resident rooms, provide abundant natural light from full-height windows, which aids orientation. Benches along the way offer places to rest, have a casual conversation, or just enjoy the view outside and the people passing by. Family rooms are available for each cluster of private rooms, where residents can meet with guests, or enjoy coffee and juice together in the mornings. The main dining room is divided into smaller dining areas for a more intimate, home-like atmosphere.

SmithGroup incorporates the outdoors at every opportunity. Each unit has outdoor space of its own, and there is a rich variety of landscaped common spaces: residents' kitchen garden, an alfresco dining courtyard, and the textural garden all encourage resident interaction and activity.

PREVIOUS: The main entry leads to the villa's main living room. **ABOVE LEFT:** Site model **ABOVE RIGHT:** The koi pond **BELOW:** Each resident room features a private balcony or patio.

ABOVE: Activity pavilions are located adjacent to the
koi pond.

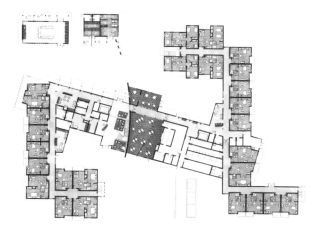

FACING PAGE: The entry lobby opens to the second floor. ABOVE: The second story dining room
DRAWING: Floor plan BELOW: Natural light streams into the single-loaded corridors.

NATIONAL ACADEMY OF SCIENCES
WASHINGTON DC 2002

The National Research Council (NRC), the operating arm of the National Academy of Sciences, the National Academy of Engineering, and the Institute of Medicine, occupies the National Academy of Sciences Building. Organized in 1916 in response to the increased need for scientific and technical services caused by World War I, NRC's primary function is to administer the studies carried out by the Academies and Institute. The building accommodates the consolidation of program units from disparate locations, achieving NRC's primary goal of creating a collaborative culture. Located on a tight urban site in downtown DC, phase I of the 581,000-square-foot facility combines offices, multi-media conferencing rooms, a library, full-service dining facilities, a lecture hall, and five levels of below-grade parking.

Within Washington, DC's strict height and design requirements, SmithGroup achieved a building design that goes well beyond mere quiet compliance. The majority of the building's square footage is tucked into the center of the block, behind a series of existing historic structures. Where the building façade edges up the sidewalk it is a good neighbor, employing limestone cladding and brick on the first four levels, reflecting the scale and rhythm of the surrounding buildings. The upper floors step back and add brick and precast concrete panels to celebrate the roof terraces, enhance the skyline, and complement the diverse styles of the neighborhood.

On the interior, a nine-story atrium visually unifies the offices and signifies connectivity. A monumental interconnecting stair links floors to promote accidental interaction among employees. The floor of the atrium is a multipurpose space devoted to social gatherings, dining, presentations, and informal meetings.

PREVIOUS: The majority of the building is tucked behind existing historic structures. ABOVE: A dichroic glass needle hangs in the atrium. BELOW: Art in the entrance lobby by Larry Kirkland depicts science, engineering, and medicine. FACING PAGE: A spiraling stair connects each level within the atrium.

CAMPUS MULTIPURPOSE BUILDING, UNIVERSITY OF CALIFORNIA, SAN DIEGO
SAN DIEGO, CALIFORNIA 2004

Driven by California's population expansion, enrollment at the University of California, San Diego is projected to increase by 10,000 students over the next decade. This growth will of course raise the demand for classroom and office space, and this need led the university to commission SmithGroup to design the Campus Multipurpose Building. The facility is located in the developing "University Center" portion of campus, a high-density zone providing student activities and interaction in support of six academic colleges. The building provides sloped-floor classrooms, computer labs, and office space for the new Sixth College Provost, as well as a significant amount of un-programmed (or surge) office space for unidentified users.

The multipurpose building's design explores the balance between creating a flexible space that will be suitable for a variety of changing users over the course of time and contributing to the growing campus community. The architect's response to this dilemma was to use a glass façade that creates an urban volume with an active street life, while promoting the kind of flexibility in interior planning that could accommodate the changes expected over the life of the project.

Other features of the building's exterior also contribute to a sense of community by encouraging interaction between the building and the site: a newly created courtyard becomes a part of a network of courtyards within the University Center; openings in the glass curtainwall reveal balconies; and a two-story glazed bridge forms part of an external circulation loop, which doubles as a sunscreen for the south façades and overlooks the courtyard and grand stairs. On the interior, structural dimensions that allow for column-free spaces and mechanical systems that can adapt to fluctuating lifecycle costs ensure flexibility.

INSET: The grand staircase in the courtyard

sixth college

P-11 PROJECT
XIAOSHAN, CHINA 2005

The Wanxiang Group, a large industrial automotive corporation, created a real estate division with the primary interest of developing the land holdings of the company. The P-11 project, a mixed-use development of retail/entertainment, office/commercial, and residential uses, is a new departure for this branch of the group, who had primarily worked with office and industrial projects. Designed as a city within a city and located adjacent to government and residential districts along one of the new boulevards of the town of Hangzhou, the project incorporates 1,000,000 square feet of retail, 50,000 square feet of office space, and three high-rise apartment buildings.

Due to zoning laws, the three distinct programmatic parts of the project were located in different parts of the site with little relationship. This compartmentalization, a common feature of much of this area of Xiaoshan, was particularly antithetical to the generation of a sense of community, which a project of this sort demands. To overcome this, SmithGroup integrated the retail section with the rest of the site. The new plan was submitted to the zoning department, who, after seeing the benefit of this type of organization, gave its approval.

The retail area consists of an internal matrix of streets and courtyards linked across the length of the site by an atrium.

At the principal intersection of the primary internal streets is the project's main circular entrance court, which is sheltered with a translucent glass and metal canopy. This space serves not only as an entrance but also as an outdoor amphitheater for performances and special events. The steel and glass twin towers of the office building, linked in the middle by an atrium, rise above the lower retail buildings, anchoring the northeast corner of the site. A garden separates and links the towers and mid-rise buildings of the residential section from the office towers and retail complex, creating a pleasant gathering space for the residents and users of P-11.

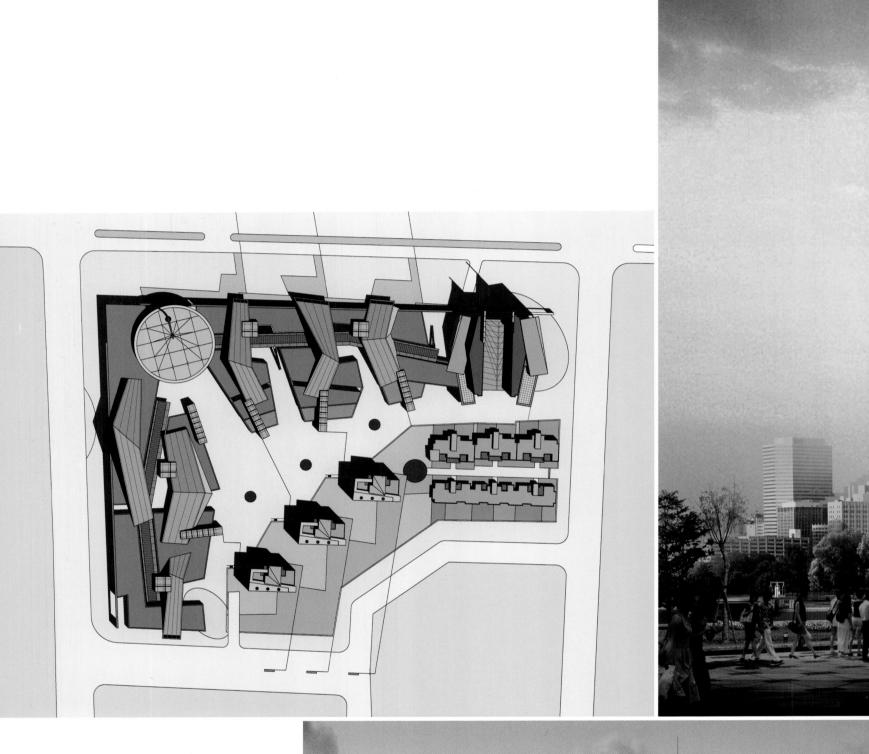

PREVIOUS: Aerial view of the P-11 Project ABOVE: Site plan
BELOW: View of the P-11 Project from the west

ABOVE: The plaza

INDIANA UNIVERSITY PURDUE UNIVERSITY INDIANAPOLIS CAMPUS CENTER
INDIANAPOLIS, INDIANA 2006

Indiana University Purdue University Indianapolis is in the process of transforming its commuter-style campus, whose scale and functions are based upon the car, into a more urban-like environment, promoting pedestrian traffic and the sense of community that goes along with it. The new campus center is a crucial part of this process because it provides a "village square"—the physical and social heart that every community needs. It is the place where visitors, students, faculty, and staff can meet friends, eat, buy books, mail a letter, cash a check, buy a ticket, see a film, or just hang out. Sited near the exact center of campus, the 250,000-square-foot center will combine a food court, bookstore, 1,000-person multipurpose room, theater, student life and diversity programs, an enrollment center, retail functions, and an array of student lounges and meeting spaces.

SmithGroup considered both the campus center's immediate surroundings and the university's envisioned goals for the campus. For example, the façade facing Michigan Street, a busy automobile thoroughfare, is composed of large-scaled elements, including a suspended glass cube, that provide a strong visual focus. In contrast, the façade facing Vermont Street, which is intended to become a pedestrian corridor, offers a major entry to the building and a vertical bell tower.

A future outdoor café is planned for this side of the building, which will tie into the interior food services. The intersection of Vermont Street and University Boulevard, at the center's corner, will be an exterior plaza, shaped for outdoor activities and events.

Inside, a glass atrium spans the length of University Boulevard and rises the full height of the building's four floors. This interior open space displays the center's functions and highlights vertical and horizontal circulation. It also offers a variety of lounge, meeting, and activity areas, where people from every corner of the campus will come together— a campus living room.

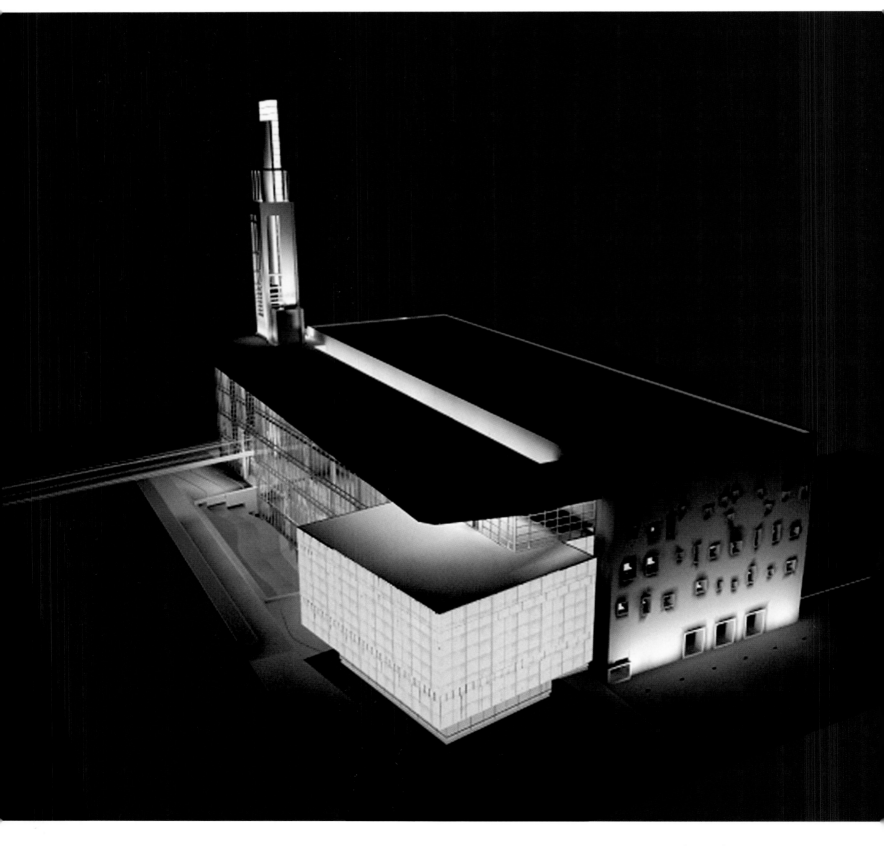

PREVIOUS: A tower marks the entrance to the center from the campus. ABOVE: A lighting study showing the suspended glass cube facing Michigan Street.

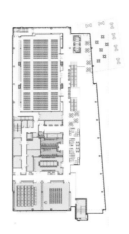

ABOVE: The atrium's interior DRAWINGS, BOTTOM TO TOP: First, second, and fourth floor plan

LAWRENCE BERKELEY NATIONAL LABORATORY
MOLECULAR FOUNDRY
BERKELEY, CALIFORNIA 2006

The Lawrence Berkeley National Laboratory, adjacent to the University of California, Berkeley campus, is the oldest Department of Energy national laboratory. It has produced nine Nobel Laureates and many revolutionary advances across the spectrum of science in its 71-year history. The molecular foundry will be a national center for nanoscience, the design,

synthesis, and characterization of materials at the molecular level. Laboratories, offices, and connecting interaction/ collaboration spaces were needed on this steeply sloped site, squeezed in between two existing buildings, with views of the San Francisco Bay and the city beyond.

The nature of laboratory design, with its many predetermined aspects, set

well-defined boundaries within which SmithGroup had to work. Clean rooms, for example, have a certain dimension, and some machinery is so sensitive to movement that it requires a seismically isolated room. The architect's scheme, a simple rectangle in plan, rises six floors above the hillside to comprise 96,000 square feet. The laboratories, which occupy 70% of

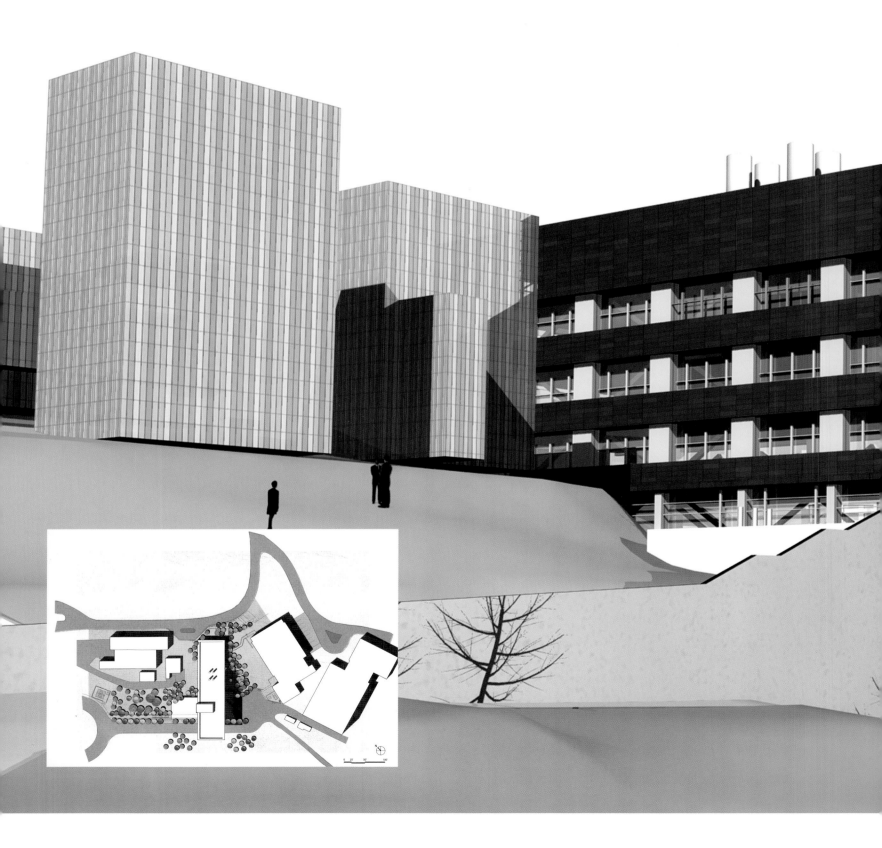

INSET: Site plan

the floor plan, were located at the eastern end of the building, which left the western end, with its views of the bay, open for the offices. A concrete plinth forms the first two stories, housing clean rooms and vibration-sensitive labs. Floors three through six are sheathed in metal panels and floor-to-ceiling glazing, and, since the laboratory spaces on these floors require exceedingly large footprints, cantilever out over the plinth to the west. Besides adding a welcome bit of drama, the cantilever also leaves room on the ground for a fire lane. Twelve-foot trusses above the roof level support the projecting mass and conceal all rooftop mechanical equipment.

The building organization links labs and offices together to create opportunities for interaction outside the lab, accommodate visitors, provide linkages with adjacent buildings, and have a thoughtful working environment for the intellectual advancement of nanoscience. The building integrates the surrounding facilities together on the hillside both functionally and visually, creating a larger community of research centers.

ABOVE: The foundry's upper four floors cantilever over the concrete plinth to the west.

3

YOU ARE HERE: ARCHITECTURE AS ICON AND MESSAGE

Many SmithGroup architects freely admit that most clients who want an icon will not come to them first, but rather choose a signature firm with a reliably flashy product. It is a source of pride, however, that SmithGroup does not have a single product to sell, but instead thoughtful buildings. Their buildings may well become icons, but rarely set out to do so. Principal Hal Davis points out that icons must emerge and cannot be dropped in from on high, immediately demanding homage.

Icon status is also reliably capricious, as the trajectory of opinion about New York's World Trade Center shows. From the day it opened in 1977, it was the built image of commercial might, then architectural and planning hubris, before finally settling into life as a dull but occasionally helpful directional. Finally and lastingly, it is an icon of national tragedy. The organic quality of this change, moving along with different tastes, attitudes toward the city, and history, is a telling (if atypical) illustration of Davis' point.

The current icon mania—even modest museums in small cities are commissioning high-octane architecture as a way of getting on the cultural map—has helped to alter the public definition of the word, pulling it in a purely formal direction. Such iconic buildings tend to be declared as such before ground is ever broken, and this undermines the possibility that a building may become one in the old-fashioned and organic sense that Davis uses, i.e., because it works and is loved. SmithGroup has designed a number of iconic buildings over the years, but their buildings tend to grow into that status because of the role each plays in its neighborhood and because of the strength of the story it tells.

The Ford Center for Environmental & Conservation Education, Detroit Zoological Institute is an interesting example of a building whose message will read so clearly that it will reinforce the idea that a building can fundamentally shape the understanding of its users. The zoo's director has a deeply held conviction that wild animals should never be treated as pets, even for educational purposes. This meant, for the SmithGroup architects working on the project, that standard zoo pedagogy had to be turned on its head along with a more typical approach to the design. The architects began with the idea that visiting schoolchildren will best understand animals if they inhabit the world of animals. SmithGroup designed a series of classrooms that are mini habitats, such as wet, polar, and desert-like. Thus, the children will learn to see themselves in a much larger spectrum of life as they move from habitat to habitat. The Ford Center's potential for shaping the way children think about the world around them is enormous and suggests that the zoo will loom large in the imagination of its young visitors. This kind of narrative power in a building is a quality that one often forgets when declaring an icon.

A more organic icon is the Discovery Communications World Headquarters in Silver Spring, Maryland. The new headquarters was intended to convey the company's philosophy of engagement and education exemplified by its Discovery Channel programs. It is no surprise that SmithGroup designed the building to light up one of the largest and historically most important corners in the downtown area. The L-shaped building's transparency and plentiful ground-level public space open it to the streets it fronts; an inflected façade and color-changing stair tower define a genuinely active public plaza in front of the lobby. What is more surprising is the effect the building has had on its neighborhood.

Silver Spring is one of the earliest of Washington, DC's suburbs, but it had once had a clear and independent identity. By the 70s, the town had fallen into decline, and this crucial site lay vacant. What makes the Discovery Headquarters a downtown icon is not so much its color and activity, but that its color and activity fill a historic hole. They remind people of the way Silver Spring's downtown once was and help to bring that lost vibrancy back to life.

Like the Ford Center, this building provides a concise working definition of the attitude so many SmithGroup architects have toward icon-making: we will provide a thoughtful building in both looks and behavior and the people who use it and see it will make it an icon.

NATIONAL POSTAL MUSEUM
WASHINGTON, DC 1993

The increasing size and complexity of American postal history and the national philatelic collections, in addition to the greater public demand for access to these materials, led two federal agencies in a joint agreement to the creation of this Smithsonian Institute museum in 1990. Located in Washington, DC's main post office building, the museum includes 25,000 square feet of exhibition space divided into five major galleries, a museum shop, a specialty shop, and a discovery center for family education and national conferences. Back-of-house spaces include a 6,000-square-foot library, a state-of-the-art paper conservation lab, exhibits preparation areas, historic collections storage,

and administrative offices. SmithGroup's design sought to express the social and technological contributions of the postal service and its role in connecting the nation within a first class museum environment. The project had to be capable of accommodating 4,000 visitors per day while maintaining secure research, curatorial, and support staff functions.

Unlike many other museums, these interiors are not a neutral canvas for the collection. Instead, they seek to reinforce the museum's message. The treatment of space, use of materials, and detailing systems are rooted in images of postal history. Wood and metal storing rooms, brass and stainless steel post office boxes, complex overhead conveyor systems,

and the rich inventory of stamps, their cancellation marks, and their graphics are the references for the design. The imagery is particularly evident in the two sales shops, with their gridded glass and metal shop fronts and their evocative overhead treatment. By contrast, the use of marble and fine wood in the central hall and atrium reflects the elegant museum tradition of the Smithsonian and is appropriate to the handsome historic lobby. The escalators that descend from this lobby are finished in engine-turned stainless steel with brass acorn caps, integrating the images of the postal service and the Smithsonian at this critical transition point.

PREVIOUS: The museum entrance and exhibit hall
ABOVE LEFT AND RIGHT: Gridded glass and metal exterior
of the museum shop BELOW: The main museum

entrance combines images of both the postal
service and the Smithsonian. FACING PAGE: Interior
of the museum shop

555 12TH STREET, NW
WASHINGTON, DC 1998

Occupying a full block in the heart of Washington, DC's central business district, 555 12th Street was built to house the city's largest law firm, Arnold & Porter. The need—both financial and urbanistic—to incorporate a large amount of retail space at the ground floor led to a program that called for 120,000 square feet of retail space and 1.1 million square feet of office space. The clients also wanted the building to fit sympathetically into an urban context that contains buildings of many eras, from early 19th-century Greek Revivalism to 1930s federal classicism and a full range of 19th- and 20th-century commercial architecture. But this sympathetic contextualism had to be balanced with an impression of modern technology and efficiency.

In response, SmithGroup designed an exterior that employs classical expressions in its overall form of base, shaft, and top, as well as in its cornices and spandrels, which invoke details often found in older commercial structures. Within this framework, the exterior detailing uses modern materials and technology to give its expressions a fresh aspect. The exterior materials and details continue partway into the interior, but are simplified and reinterpreted to make a transition to the strictly modern great atrium. This soaring cylindrical space, 11 stories high, is ringed with glass and metal and vertically accentuated by tall thin columns and aluminum mullions. At its apex is a skylight, which suffuses the interior with light during the day. At night a translucent ring of glass, suspended from a fretwork of steel trusses, provides a halo of light.

PREVIOUS: Daylight pours into the atrium through the glass ceiling. FACING PAGE: The 12th Street entrance ABOVE LEFT: View of the atrium from the 11th Street

entrance ABOVE RIGHT: The building's bay windows BELOW: The building employs classical expressions in its overall form of base, shaft, and top.

555 12TH STREET, NW   83

ABOVE LEFT: Interior of main lobby **ABOVE RIGHT:** Balconies on the 11th and 12th floors of the atrium **BELOW:** View to 12th Street from the atrium

ABOVE: The translucent ring of glass hanging above the atrium is illuminated at night.

555 12TH STREET, NW

85

MCI CENTER
WASHINGTON, DC 1998

The MCI Center, home to the NBA's Washington Wizards, the NHL's Washington Capitals, and the WNBA's Washington Mystics, is located in the heart of historic Washington, DC. The building is adjacent to Chinatown and faces the classical edifices of the National Portrait Gallery and the National Museum of American Art.

SmithGroup, which was in charge of the exterior design of this 20,300-seat arena, faced the challenge of creating a distinctly modern structure in this predominantly historical district. The architects' solution was to pay extraordinarily close attention to scale, so that a contemporary vocabulary could become a contribution to a richly varied neighborhood, and not the clothing on a massive intruder. The MCI Center's four distinctly articulated façades respond to the differing urban characters of each side. Height and cornice detail coincide with the street line of monumental buildings along F Street. The carefully detailed surface wall is punctuated by large window openings on three sides to allow visibility inside and outside of the various activities. The façade is also highlighted by a series of large-scale sculptural elements that orient the building and focus its relationship to each side of the city. The main F Street entry features a large portico referencing the entry portals of the National Portrait Gallery. Sign towers on the centerline of G Street reference the alignment of the L'Enfant Plan, while stylized medallions of the plan grace the building at various points. A serpentine dragon canopy on the northwest corner of the building gives a nod to Chinatown, as does a pagoda-like portico, and an elaborate Chinese figure symbolizing long life is woven into the brick pattern. While these details pay homage to the architectural context, the combined use of steel, glass, and masonry distinguish the building as a late 20th-century composition.

ARCHITECTURE AS ICON AND MESSAGE

PREVIOUS: The southwest corner ABOVE: The center
seen from the west BELOW: The portico of the
F Street entrance references the entrance portals of

the National Portrait Gallery. FACING PAGE:
The north façade of the center reflects the influence
of Washington's Chinatown.

體育中心

NATIONAL MUSEUM OF NATURAL HISTORY, WEST COURT RENOVATION
WASHINGTON, DC 1998

The National Museum of Natural History, one of the Smithsonian Institution museums located along the National Mall in Washington, DC, planned an infill and renovation for its central courtyard. The program featured a 487-seat, 3-D IMAX theater, an educational discovery center for interactive exhibits, kitchens and a 600-seat café, and lateral connection bridges to span the six-story circulation atrium. In all, the project comprised 75,000 square feet. SmithGroup served as a consulting architect to HGA and was responsible for the design of the public spaces and restaurant surrounding the IMAX theater. The primary goal was to integrate the new elements with the existing landmark building in a way that maintained the building's clarity and monumental character, but the new elements had to be specific to the architecture of the museum and reflect its substance and character. The architects achieved this both in their use of forms and materials. For example, the atrium stair, which is totally self-supporting so as not to strain the existing structure, invokes the notion of armature and spine and suggests vertebrate zoology. Floor patterns throughout the project connote abstract leaves and other earth-related motifs. The finish materials of travertine and limestone actually contain fossils. Light fixtures are crystalline and mineral in character.

The design responds to the vertical organization of the original building with the café at the basement level, the theater entrance at the piano nobile level, and the theater exit at the second floor. The discovery center is at the highest level, just below the skylight and overlooking the atrium. The café is organized as a circular form within a basic cruciform shape evocative of beaux-arts symmetrical formalism and reminiscent of the rotunda dome, while the discovery center offers views of both the original atrium walls and the new, beaux-arts inspired truss work.

ARCHITECTURE AS ICON AND MESSAGE

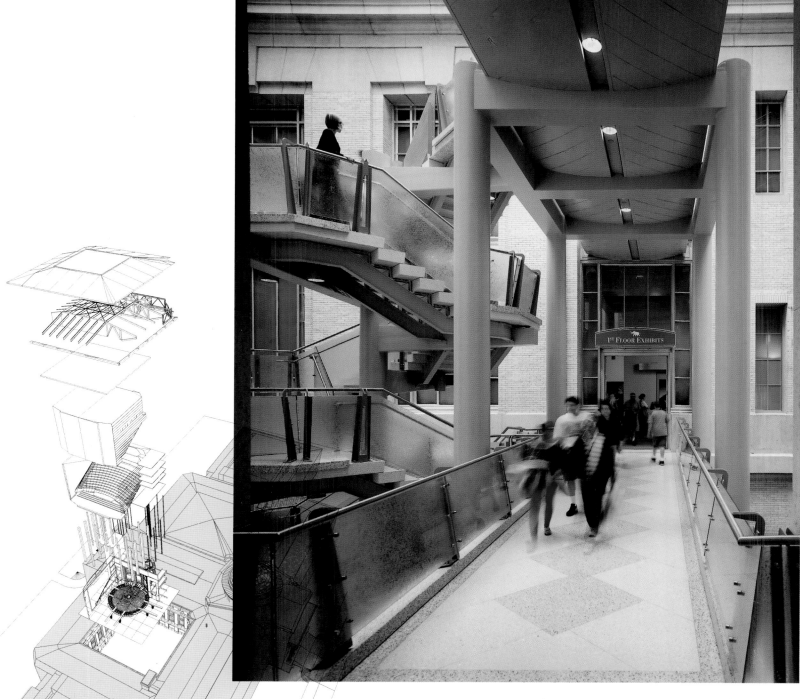

ARCHITECTURE AS ICON AND MESSAGE

PREVIOUS: The atrium stair is self-supporting so as not to strain the existing structure. ABOVE: The IMAX theater BELOW: Lateral connection bridges

improve circulation through the atrium. DRAWING: Exploded axonometric FACING PAGE: Café tables occupy the atrium floor.

SMITHGROUP DETROIT OFFICE RELOCATION
DETROIT, MICHIGAN 1999

The Detroit, Michigan office relocation of SmithGroup involved the renovation of 70,000 square feet of the second, 17th, 18th, 19th, and 20th floors of the Guardian Building in the heart of downtown. Originally designed in 1929 for the Union Trust Bank by one of SmithGroup's predecessor firms, Smith Hinchman & Grylls, the building represents the height of Art Deco

in Detroit for its elaborate tile, stone, and terra-cotta exterior, as well as for the ornate tile, marble, and travertine interior. The main banking hall, on the second floor, was even imagined as a "cathedral of finance," with a traditional basilica form, high vaulted nave, and side "chapels," all finished in elaborate ornamentation, painted murals, and painted canvas ceiling.

The objective of the new design was to insert new spaces and technology into the existing structure without detracting from or competing with the grandeur of the original design concept. For example, in the nave of the main banking hall, two conference rooms were conceived as simple, finely crafted, contemporary objects that appear almost as temporary constructions. Each

uses a series of components that could be easily disassembled, leaving the original space untouched. They are constructed out of clear and ribbed translucent glass, back-lit to reinforce a sense of lightness, and fastened to a painted steel frame with clearly visible through-bolt connections. The palette is intentionally neutral and background in character. From inside the

conference room, one can see up through a perforated steel and glass roof to the original painted Art Deco ceiling, which is illuminated with hidden up-lighting.

Floors 17 through 20 are organized in relation to the building massing, which features a square north section and an octagonal south section joined by a long rectangular section. The octagonal section

houses administrative spaces, including clerical workstations, glass-enclosed offices, and video conference rooms. The square northern area houses special functiwons, such as accounting, computer services, libraries, kitchenettes, and quiet rooms. The rectangular area is an open studio space with a loop aisle system, and an open space as a center for informal collaboration.

PREVIOUS: The conference rooms and offices almost appear as temporary constructions. LEFT: A conference room RIGHT: The Guardian building in the 1930s FACING PAGE: Office suites

INDIANA UNIVERSITY SCHOOL OF LAW, LAWRENCE W. INLOW HALL
INDIANAPOLIS, INDIANA 2001

Lawrence W. Inlow Hall, a new facility for the Indiana University School of Law, Indianapolis, rests on an important corner site. Comprising a 70,000-square-foot law library, 68,000 square feet housing offices and a law clinic, and 47,000 square feet of classrooms and student spaces, the building is the first view of the campus to pedestrian and vehicular traffic coming from downtown and the state capitol complex three blocks away. The southern façade faces historic Military Park, the eastern façade faces West Street, a major urban thoroughfare, and

the northern façade faces a future academic quadrangle. The building had to become a new landmark to anchor this significant corner of campus in downtown Indianapolis, and provide direction for the future quadrangle.

The resulting design from SmithGroup gave strong formal identity to the major program elements of the law school by associating them with the distinguishing site characteristics. For example, the law library, which runs along West Street, is composed of large-scale elements including a reading room and stair tower.

Faculty, student services, and clinical offices were placed behind an articulated curtainwall to form a transparent, permeable screen along Military Park. The building's formal entry also addresses the park. Building and landscape elements form an appropriately scaled, welcoming courtyard for the façade facing the academic quadrangle. The monumental, transparent reading room at the corner of West Street and Military Park presents a welcoming beacon to those approaching the campus, and is symbolic of the life of inquiry within the law school and the entire university.

PREVIOUS: The monumental, transparent reading room is a welcoming beacon for those approaching the campus. ABOVE LEFT: Moot courtroom

ABOVE RIGHT: Dining courtyard BELOW: A welcoming courtyard faces the future campus quadrangle. FACING PAGE: The atrium

21000 ATLANTIC BOULEVARD, DULLES TOWN CENTER BUILDING ONE
DULLES, VIRGINIA 2002

Lerner Enterprises, an experienced developer in the Washington, DC, area, commissioned this 175,000-square-foot, seven-story structure of speculative office space sited on 12.5 acres of the Dulles Town Center master plan, which includes offices, retail locations, restaurants, a shopping mall, and residential plots. This area of Northern Virginia is rapidly developing as a worldwide nucleus of information technology and consequently has a tenant base of high-tech firms. The project offered SmithGroup an opportunity to explore the dynamic relationship between the more traditional world of brick-and-mortar architecture and the modern realm of digital technology.

The site is bordered by Route 28, a high-speed vehicular corridor, on its long, western edge. To the east lie Atlantic Boulevard and the town center proper. These contrasting environments established a "split personality" for the building, which the architects exploited as a way of making what could have been a generic project highly specific to its site. The west façade responds to the high-speed movement of the highway with its smooth, folded stainless steel-coated curtainwall and abstracted metallic appearance. In contrast, the east façade is an ordered grid of precast concrete with punched openings that responds to the civic realm of the town center. The building's bifurcation, however, is not so simple. Each façade bears elements of its opposite. The east façade is punctuated with a folded, glazed entrance tower, while a monumental window and projecting cube appear on the west.

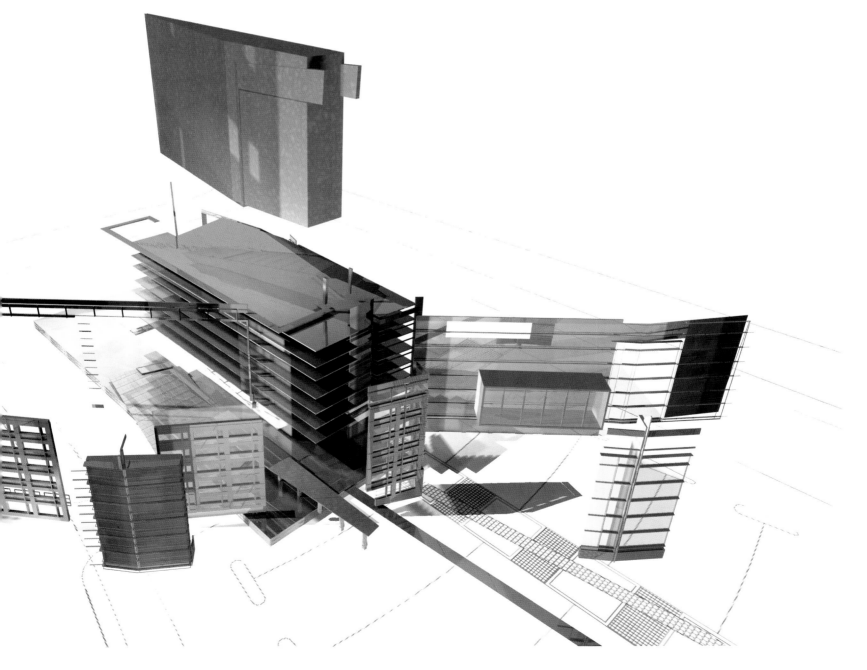

PREVIOUS: The building's "split personality" features
a smooth glass curtainwall on the west façade and an
ordered grid of precast concrete on the east.

FACING PAGE: Detail of the west façade ABOVE LEFT:
The east façade ABOVE RIGHT: The monumental window
of the west façade DRAWING: Exploded axonometric

21000 ATLANTIC BOULEVARD   105

HANGZHOU MUNICIPAL CENTER (COMPETITION)
HANGZHOU, CHINA 2002

Located in the new central business district of Hangzhou, China, the new municipal center is situated in the middle of an urban park zoned for civic, cultural, and environmental venues for the people of the city. The center accommodates all of the functions of the central government for the city and its provincial district, such as offices, meeting and reception rooms, assembly halls, and court chambers in a single volume. The site is divided into two halves by the building, each symbolic of the primary natural resources of the region. To the east, a large water park extends to the river, recalling the historic West Lake. To the west, tree-lined and contoured landscaping recalls the mountains that surround the city. The city's financial and commercial districts lie to the north and south respectively, and the building acts as a connector between the two.

The design of the 240,000-square-meter, 26-floor building acts both as a window and as a bridge. SmithGroup decided to create links—both visual and physical—between the water and land: the large reflecting pool which mirrors the glazed façade is fed by a thin channel leading to the bay. The structure also houses large assembly spaces beneath the contoured landscaping to the west and beneath the reflecting pool. The east and west glass façades, which, depending on the time of day, create both reflective and transparent backdrops to the city, are punctured to form a formal entrance court that also creates views through the building to the landscaping or the water.

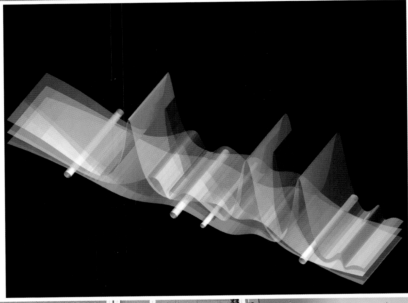

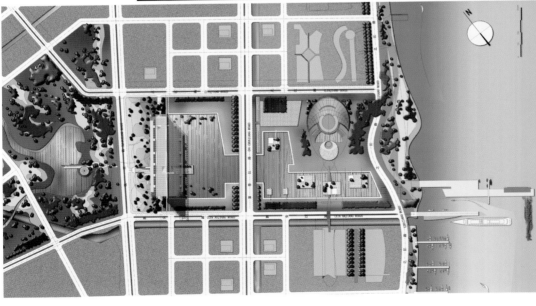

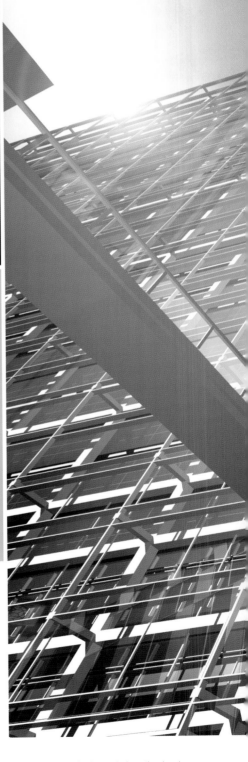

ARCHITECTURE AS ICON AND MESSAGE

PREVIOUS: A large reflecting pool mirrors the glazed façade. **ABOVE:** A view of the plaza **MIDDLE:** Site diagram **BELOW:** Site plan

DISCOVERY COMMUNICATIONS WORLD HEADQUARTERS
SILVER SPRING, MARYLAND 2003

The offices of Discovery Communications, a privately held, diversified media company that provides cable television programming, online services, and retail stores, were scattered throughout several buildings in Bethesda, Maryland. The company wanted to consolidate its departments into one headquarters facility that would include offices, screening and conference rooms, and event facilities, while communicating its commitment to exploration, learning, and community involvement. Occupying a previously empty 3.4-acre, triangular site adjacent to

the inter modal transit center and at Silver Spring's major crossroads, the project is a significant element in the redevelopment of one of Washington, DC's oldest near-suburban neighborhoods.

The 580,000-square-foot, L-shaped structure stands as the major gateway and landmark of downtown Silver Spring as well as a center for community life. SmithGroup took advantage of the centrality of the site and designed a building it can comfortably hold. The main façades of stone and glass front the two main public thoroughfares, and, on

the inverse side, form a ceremonial entry. Cradled between the arms of the building are the half-acre Discovery Plaza, and the one-acre Discovery Garden. These public spaces link to the transit center and knit the headquarters into the fabric of the neighborhood's civic life. The main lobby, a ten-story atrium at the juncture of the building's two arms, provides space for exhibits, while a mural by Narcissus Quagliata takes advantage of the opportunity for public art along the building's exterior.

ARCHITECTURE AS ICON AND MESSAGE

PREVIOUS: Discovery Plaza knits the headquarters into the fabric of the neighborhood's civic life.
ABOVE: The main entrance at night

ABOVE: Detail of the northeast façade
BELOW: The atrium's exterior as seen from
the roof garden

ABOVE: A building detail as seen from the plaza
BELOW: Interior of the public lobby **FACING PAGE:**
A ten-story atrium joins the building's two arms.

FREEDOM FIELDS
LEXINGTON, MISSOURI 2003

Located outside of Lexington, Missouri, an antebellum town that is home to a Civil War battlefield, Freedom Fields is intended to help close the knowledge gap between the public and the military. Commissioned by the National Military Education Center, the 75,000-square-foot core facility on a 120-acre site perched over the Missouri River will be the hub of an emerging campus comprising a conference center, lodging facilities, educational spaces, and possibly a

Center for Excellence for Homeland Security and Defense. The facility establishes a new model in learning environments that will blend exhibits and simulation and interactive laboratories to teach leadership and team building. The surrounding site will include fitness trails, obstacle courses, and room for military re-enactments. The education and exhibit components will focus on leadership, diplomacy, and military history, with an emphasis on its social

impact and evolution.

Rammed earth, glass, and steel comprise an architectural vocabulary that draws from the military lexicon but is seamless with the exhibit and educational areas. In addition to metaphoric references, the building's design engages the site, its views, and distinctive terrain via a solid front façade and a transparent back façade that opens to the forested hillside and view over the river shed.

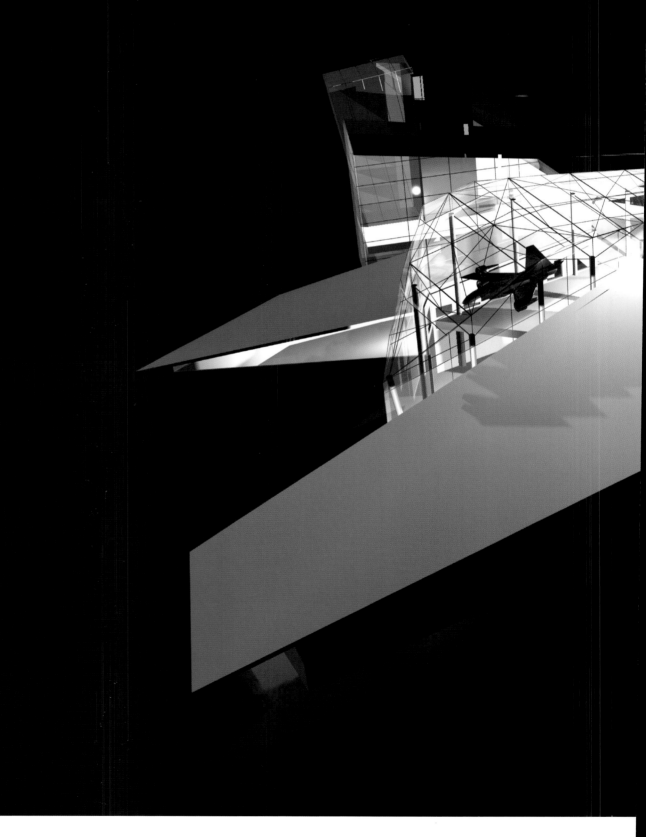

ABOVE: Axonometric rendering of the museum and learning center

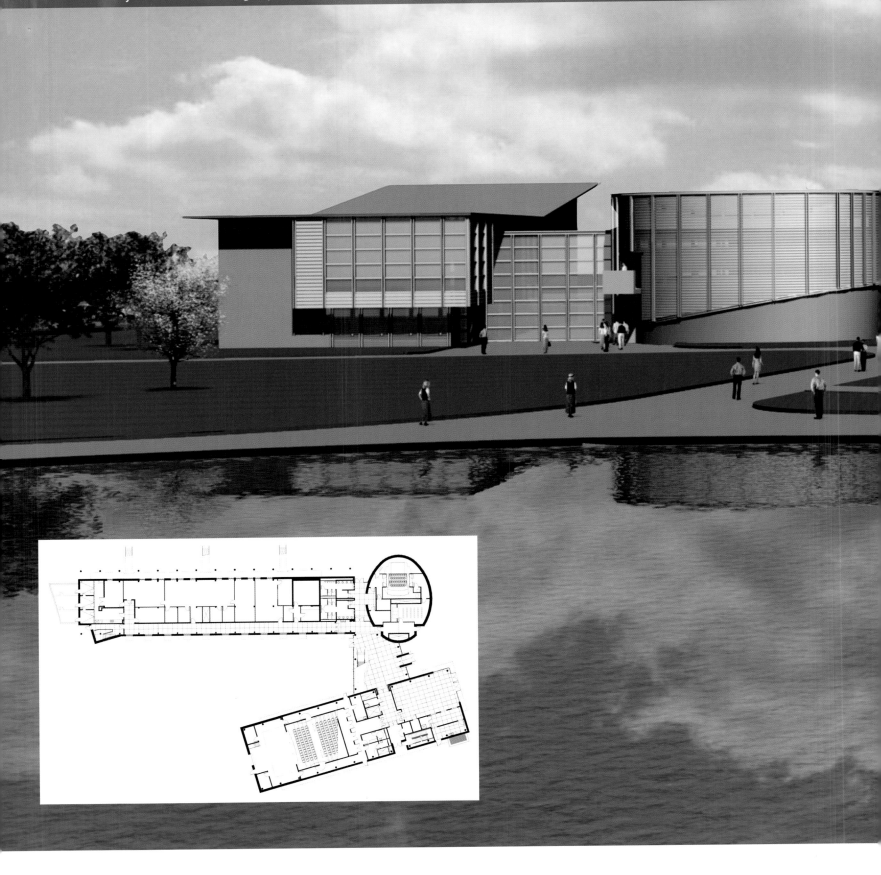

FORD CENTER FOR ENVIRONMENTAL & CONSERVATION EDUCATION, DETROIT ZOOLOGICAL INSTITUTE ROYAL OAK, MICHIGAN 2004

The Detroit Zoo, one of the finest zoological institutions in the country, needed a new home for its educational department. They chose a three-acre site on an existing picnic area within the 125-acre zoological park. The 40,000-square-foot center was designed primarily to accommodate the many hundreds of school groups that visit every year. The facility contains six classrooms, as well as a small discovery area, space for administrative functions and volunteer services, and a 250-seat, multi-use theatre with an accompanying gallery space and dining facility. Special amenities include the Wild Adventure Simulator, an audio, visual, and motion adventure ride, and an arena for live animals.

In thinking about the Ford Center, architects at the SmithGroup took the director's commitment to animal conservation as inspiration and designed a participatory immersion experience meant to generate a heightened awareness of our responsibility to protecting wildlife in a way that

INSET: First floor plan

any child can understand. Each classroom has a theme (drippy place, cold place, etc.) and simulates that particular ecosystem's lighting, sound, and climate, and on entering each room, the children get a visceral sense of what life might be like as an animal. These rooms also house a series of 25-square-foot terrarium/ aquariums, containing animals found in these habitats. Two of the rooms are further specialized: a wet laboratory and an art room. The theater continues the idea of immersion through its use of materials. The concrete floors and columns, the olive-colored concrete masonry walls and wood siding, and the wood trusses and roof deck provide a visually stimulating backdrop for performances. The seating and carpet here are even synthetic, colorful adaptations of animal skins, a reference to the reliance we have always had on animals for our clothing and shelter.

DOWNTOWN YMCA
DETROIT, MICHIGAN 2005

SmithGroup designed this YMCA for a 1.43-acre urban brown-field site in downtown Detroit. Situated in the northeast section of the central business district, the site is crossed by People Mover tracks and is within walking distance from Comerica Park, Ford Field, and the newly emerging entertainment district. The 100,000-square-foot building accommodates three major components: fitness, childcare, and arts and humanities, along with the requisite support spaces. A warm water pool, leisure pool, and four-lane lap pool; a full basketball court, two racquetball courts, and 1/13-mile banked indoor running track;

exercise equipment, weight machines, and free weights; and two aerobic rooms comprise the fitness component. The childcare component includes a short-term Child-Watch area, along with a fully licensed all-day childcare center for children two to five years old, and a private charter school program for kindergarteners. A 225-seat black-box style theater, a family arts center, and classrooms for media, literary, and visual arts comprise the arts and humanities component. Support spaces include men's, women's, and special needs locker rooms, massage/spa area, member's lounge, branch offices, and the main lobby.

This will be the first YMCA in the country to house all of these functions in one building.

The architectural expression of the Downtown YMCA can be thought of as a series of "tubes," into which the programmatic elements were arranged and stacked one atop the other to form split-level floors. While brick defines the core elements, and ground-face block at the entrance lends a sense of solidity, metal paneling balances out the effect and glass curtainwalls open up views. Due to the use of glass and the split-level floors throughout the building views are available to rooms above and below, as well as to the exterior.

PREVIOUS: The main entrance ABOVE: The Detroit People Mover passes through the YMCA's urban site.

YMCA SITE

GRAND RIVER AVE.

FARMER ST.

JOHN R ST.

BROADWAY AVE.

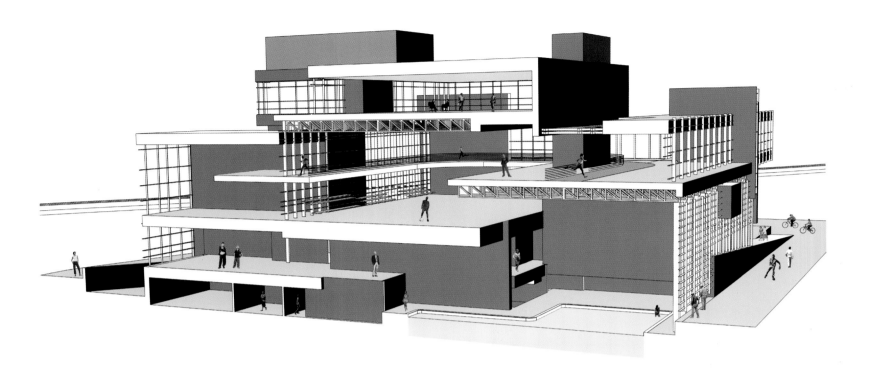

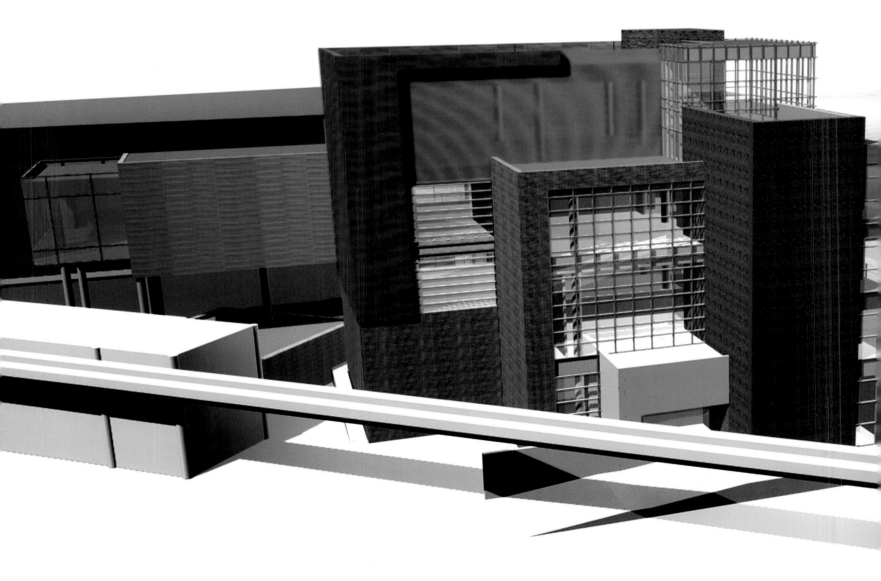

ARCHITECTURE AS ICON AND MESSAGE

ABOVE: Due to the use of glass and the split-level floors throughout the building, views are available to rooms above and below, as well as to the exterior.
BELOW: Southwest elevation

ABOVE: Section through the theater, athletic facility, classrooms, and lobby

4

GROUNDWORK: INNOVATION AND ANALYSIS

Architecture magazines would have their readers believe that innovation is primarily formal: the blobs that ruled their pages a few years back heralded a curvaceous new world, and the folds that have supplanted them declare that the future will look a lot like a piece of ribbon candy. These new forms only stick, however, when there is something actually new and valuable in the thinking behind them and if they can exert a pull on our imagination strong enough to influence the ways we think about the spaces around us. Innovators, from Joseph Paxton to Charles and Ray Eames and on, first attract us with beautiful forms, but keep us because they widen our thinking about architecture and the ways we can use it.

One of SmithGroup's most groundbreaking projects is their building for the Chesapeake Bay Foundation (CBF), a conservation organization dedicated to saving the Chesapeake Bay watershed. The CBF asked SmithGroup to design a building that would embody their ideals not just metaphorically, but physically. The architects thus adopted a "cradle-to-cradle" philosophy, meaning the building is made from recycled materials, which can be recycled again at the end of their useful lives, closing the loop. Its internal systems are based on the same philosophy: from thermal mass heating and cooling to toilets that compost, the building's impact on the land around it is minimal.

When the CBF building was published and became widely known, it gave resolve to ecologically well-meaning but skeptical architects everywhere. Finally, there was an example of a truly green project that was actually good-looking; the project helped to banish once and for all the reputation of ecologically responsible buildings as joyless, clumsy, and incompatible with good design. This marriage of style and green-ness, of philosophy and form, has turned the foundation's offices into a de-facto museum. So many people request to visit it—conservationists and architects alike—that there are now several groups walking through it every day. SmithGroup pushed the existing body of knowledge on green design further than it had ever gone, and made it seem like the reasonable thing to do.

Just as the Chesapeake Bay Foundation built on (and then transformed) earlier technological innovations, another project in the works is pushing the boundaries of an older method to a completely new level. In a project for the Kaiser Permanente Company, SmithGroup has brought the Eamsian idea of the "kit of parts" up to a large and complex architectural scale.

The Kaiser Permanente Hospital system had recently moved toward a business model that would standardize hospital upgrades and construction across California to keep costs down and speed up the construction process. In the past, the company had used templates for individual elements, such as labs and nurses stations, but each facility as a whole was treated separately. SmithGroup's new template includes basic architectural and engineering criteria and documentation that can be adjusted to many different site conditions, while keeping the central plan elements consistent. The innovations are ones of process rather than form, because the template is one that prescribes delivery as well as design vocabulary. In fact, SmithGroup and its joint venture partner, Gordon Chong and Partners, are designing three of the first facilities implementing the new template.

Kaiser Permanente is a not-for-profit, but that doesn't change the fact that it is selling a product and must keep up to date with the changing needs of its community. Speed and flexibility in delivering that product are as important in healthcare as in any other business. SmithGroup's success in developing a new process for delivering a working design is as crucial to the long-term health of the architectural profession as any formal innovation.

U.S. DEPARTMENT OF ENERGY, NEVADA SUPPORT FACILITY
NORTH LAS VEGAS, NEVADA 1997

The United States Department of Energy (DOE) Nevada is the administrative component of the Nevada Test Site, which is primarily responsible for DOE Defense Programs. Test site activity encompasses nuclear weapons initiatives, non-proliferation verification, and arms reduction processing.

During the design process of this administrative headquarters, SmithGroup helped DOE Nevada to redefine its corporate culture from a windowless and restricted closed office environment to one which nurtures the individual with daylight and views in a team setting.

To minimize the structure's height and reduce western exposure, the architects tucked the three-story, 164,000-square-foot building into the sloping site, which abuts upon a residential neighborhood. Screen walls and courtyards diminish the massing and offer shelter from solar heat gain, while a landscaped berm with native plants further mitigates the views to and from the site. The south campus drive was enhanced to provide a sense of entry for the public.

Four major functions delineate the diagram of the facility: an open public lobby and ancillary meeting and dining spaces, the security control point, the secure office functions, and the Q clearance classified areas. Security procedures required that areas stack vertically and that secure space not communicate directly with less-secure space. Thus, the Q clearance classified areas were located in wings set perpendicular to the secure portion of the building, which allowed light and views to the internal open office space.

PREVIOUS: A detail of the support facility
LEFT AND RIGHT: Shading differs according to
the building's orientation to the sun.

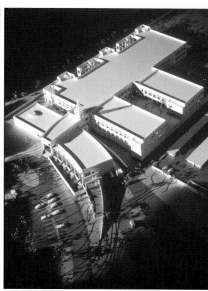

ABOVE LEFT: The site's landscaping includes native plants.
ABOVE RIGHT: Site model

NEVADA SUPPORT FACILITY   131

PHILIP MERRILL ENVIRONMENTAL CENTER

PREVIOUS: Rainwater collection cisterns
ABOVE: The center as seen from Black Walnut Creek
DRAWING: First floor plan

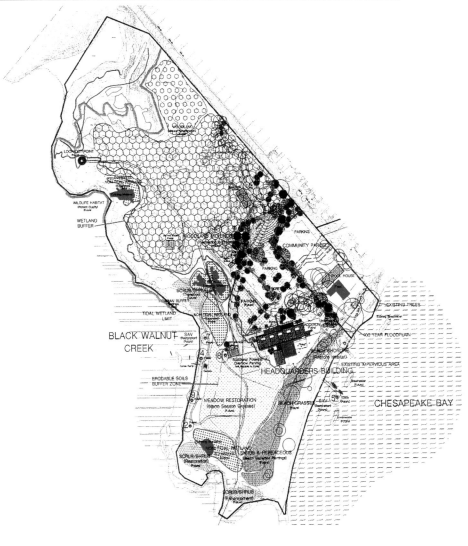

ABOVE: The center sits on concrete piers located over the footprint of a previous building. DRAWING: Site plan

CHESAPEAKE BAY FOUNDATION   137

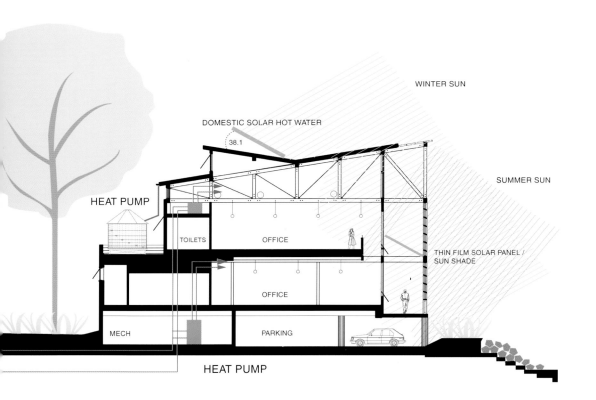

WINTER SUN

DOMESTIC SOLAR HOT WATER

38.1

HEAT PUMP

SUMMER SUN

TOILETS   OFFICE

THIN FILM SOLAR PANEL / SUN SHADE

OFFICE

MECH   PARKING

HEAT PUMP

LEFT: The main lobby and corridor to office areas
RIGHT: The main lobby as seen from above

DRAWING: Section showing climactic analysis FACING
PAGE: A trellised walkway runs along the south façade.

ABOVE: The center as seen from the south

SHANGHAI MUNICIPAL ELECTRIC POWER COMPANY HEADQUARTERS (COMPETITION)
PUDONG, SHANGHAI, CHINA 2001

This invited competition, which included an international field of four teams, was developed to provide the municipal electric utility in Shanghai with a new executive headquarters, technical monitoring facilities, a conferencing facility, and tradeshow exhibit spaces. The project occupies a triangular site located along the main road in the Pudong district (a primarily commercial area that has been under intense development over the past 15 years), where an existing 29-story, 370,000-square-foot concrete-framed tower was abandoned with only its primary structure complete. Besides completing the tower, the design had to provide an additional 100,000 square

feet to house the monitoring, conference, and exhibit facilities. All of the built space needed to be conscious of concerns linked to the business of energy and of the history of the site.

SmithGroup's winning design proposes several ideas to make full use of the site's potential and to reinforce the energy company's operations. For example, in order to strengthen the relationship of the building to the street, the new program was placed in four-story plinth buildings that border the edges of the triangle formed by Century and Yen Shen Roads. This then created a large courtyard between the two plinth buildings, providing a welcoming entry sequence for both

vehicles and pedestrians. The circulation sequence within the complex itself moves the visitor, the employee, and the executive alike through a series of experiences that tell the story of Shanghai Power Company's critical role in the urbanization of the city and its region.

The design also uses energy and light as both aesthetic elements in the lighting of the building and in a number of energy-conscious applications. A double façade, the exploration of photovoltaic materials on the roof, and the proposal of an energy co-generation plan on the site to serve the immediate district all combine to make the complex a vivid exemplar of the possibilities of the future of the energy business.

PREVIOUS: The headquarters at night
ABOVE: Axonometric rendering

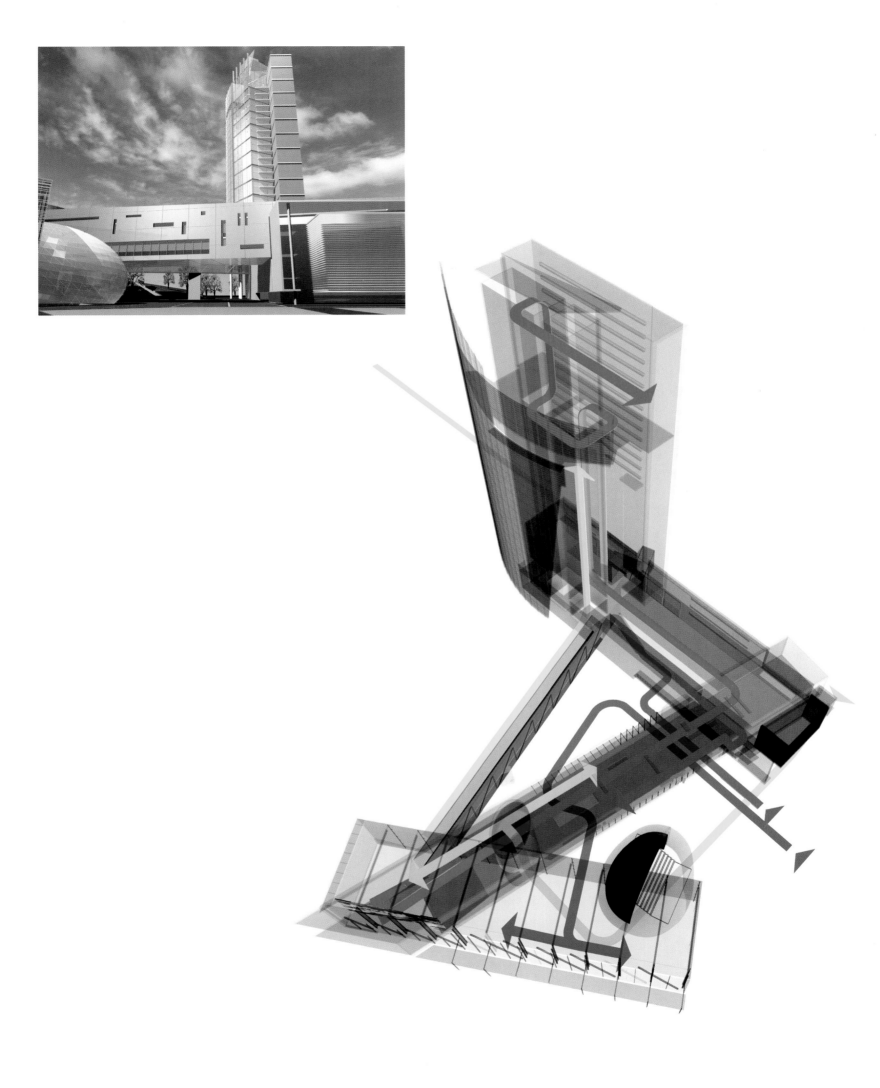

LEFT: The entrance is located between the two plinth buildings. RIGHT: The circulatory experience paths

MCNAMARA TERMINAL/NORTHWEST WORLDGATEWAY, DETROIT METROPOLITAN AIRPORT
ROMULUS, MICHIGAN 2002

Northwest Airlines, the United States' fourth largest passenger airline, required a new hub at Detroit Metropolitan Airport to service approximately 30 million passengers per year. The ambitious building program included 97 gates for both domestic and international flights, along with the ability to expand, 106 ticketing positions, a premier international arrivals hall, and large hold rooms. In addition, Northwest wanted the Federal Inspection Services area to be able to

process 3,200 international passengers per hour—the equivalent of eight 747 jets arriving simultaneously—to help the airline achieve a 31-minute average connection time between international and domestic flights.

While air travel has come to be seen as a hassle, SmithGroup aimed to make the interior of the terminal a unique and architecturally exciting environment that gives passengers a reason to pause and enjoy the sights and sounds. The

center link, which joins the terminal with Concourse A, is a soaring 70-foot-high, clerestory-lit space lined with some 80 shops and restaurants. As passengers emerge from the link onto the concourse they are presented with a 39-foot-diameter, black granite water feature designed by the internationally renowned firm Wet Design. Forty-five laminar streams, lit by fiber-optic lights that change in color, create a kinetic, choreographed display that varies from

tranquilly contemplative to playfully energetic. Behind the water feature, 18-foot-tall windows showcase the noses of visiting 747s.

The site was challenging: a 314-acre midfield location, confined by four active runways. It led SmithGroup to design a main concourse of two long wings, laid end-to-end, to create a nearly a one-mile-long expanse of both domestic and international jet gates. Concourse A, where 64 of the 97 gates are located,

is 4,900 feet in length.

While the elongated shape makes it easy for passengers to remain oriented in the expansive complex, it required an innovative mechanism to move passengers down its length in a timely fashion. To solve this problem, SmithGroup brought an automated people mover system into the concourse in the form of two sleek red trains, capable of carrying 200 passengers each, that quietly move on cushions of air just 21 feet above

the passengers on the mezzanine level. This Express Tram moves 3,900 feet, with a stop at the center link and at each end, in just two and a half minutes.

An 800-foot passenger tunnel, connecting the east and west concourses, offers travelers a mood-enhancing light and sound experience. Sculpted glass panels, LED lighting, and choreographed music and sounds give passengers who pass through the tunnel a welcome respite from the hurries of travel.

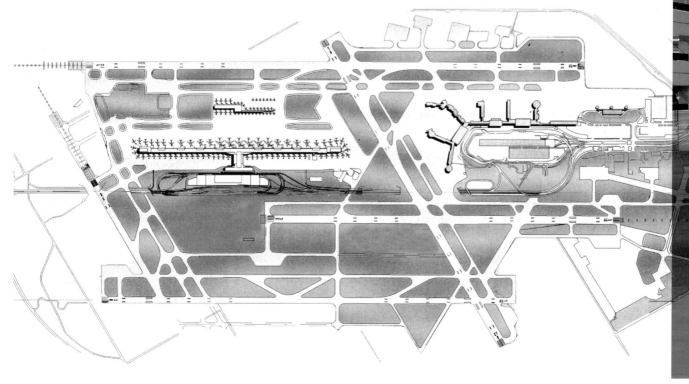

PREVIOUS: The terminal's passenger tunnel is a mood-enhancing orchestration of light, motion, and sound. ABOVE: The terminal entrance BELOW: The terminal's two wings form a nearly one-mile-long expanse of gates. DRAWING: Site plan

ABOVE: Departing passengers arrive under a broad
cantilevered canopy. BELOW: The entrance offers three
access levels.

ABOVE LEFT: The ticketing area ABOVE RIGHT: Along the mezzanine of Concourse A, the express tram moves quietly on a cushion of air. BELOW: Forty-five laminar streams, lit by fiber-optic lights that change in color, comprise the water feature's kinetic display. FACING PAGE: The center link connects the ticketing area with the main concourse.

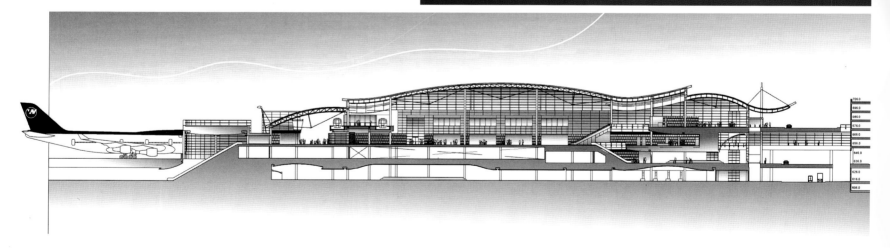

ABOVE LEFT: The 800-foot tunnel offers passengers a soothing sensory experience. ABOVE RIGHT: Detail of a sand-carved laminated glass panel

DRAWING: Section through main concourse
FACING PAGE: The tunnel features sculpted art glass panels, LED lighting, and custom music.

MCNAMARA TERMINAL/NORTHWEST WORLDGATEWAY

Gate
A33

DTW Press

Gate
A31

Gate
A29

Gate
A27

Gate
A25

Gate
A23

↑ Gates A1 to A23 →

↑ Gates A1 to A23 →

EXIT

ABOVE: The main concourse features a neutral palette of terrazzo, stainless steel, glass, and granite, which

NATIONAL RENEWABLE ENERGY LABORATORY, SCIENCE & TECHNOLOGY FACILITY
GOLDEN, COLORADO 2005

The research mission of the United States Department of Energy's National Renewable Energy Laboratory (NREL) is to reduce energy consumption and to diminish the reliance of the U.S. on fossil fuels through innovative and accessible strategies. Sited on the southern slope of Table Mountain, where the prairie meets the Rocky Mountains, the new 71,000-square-foot Science & Technology Facility (S&TF) will support advanced scientific investigation in photovoltaic and thin film applications.

SmithGroup architects pragmatically accommodated the program requirements by housing each of the two main components—offices and laboratories—in separate volumes, connecting them with a vertical entry lobby.

In support of the NREL's mission to promote sustainable buildings and energy conservation, all laboratory and office spaces in the facility were engineered to achieve a LEED™ silver rating, utilize natural daylight, and promote views of the natural setting. The "butterfly" roof above the single-level office block provides daylight from the north and south and demonstrates water harvesting. The open office environment enjoys views through the transparent perimeter offices and via a large north-facing window that frames the slope of Table Mountain. The two-level lab is illuminated from north- and south-facing clerestories. Here, too, a north-facing window focuses upon the mountain scenery. The architects carefully placed all fenestration to optimize the appropriate amount of daylight without negatively impacting the building's energy consumption.

ABOVE: A model of the facility

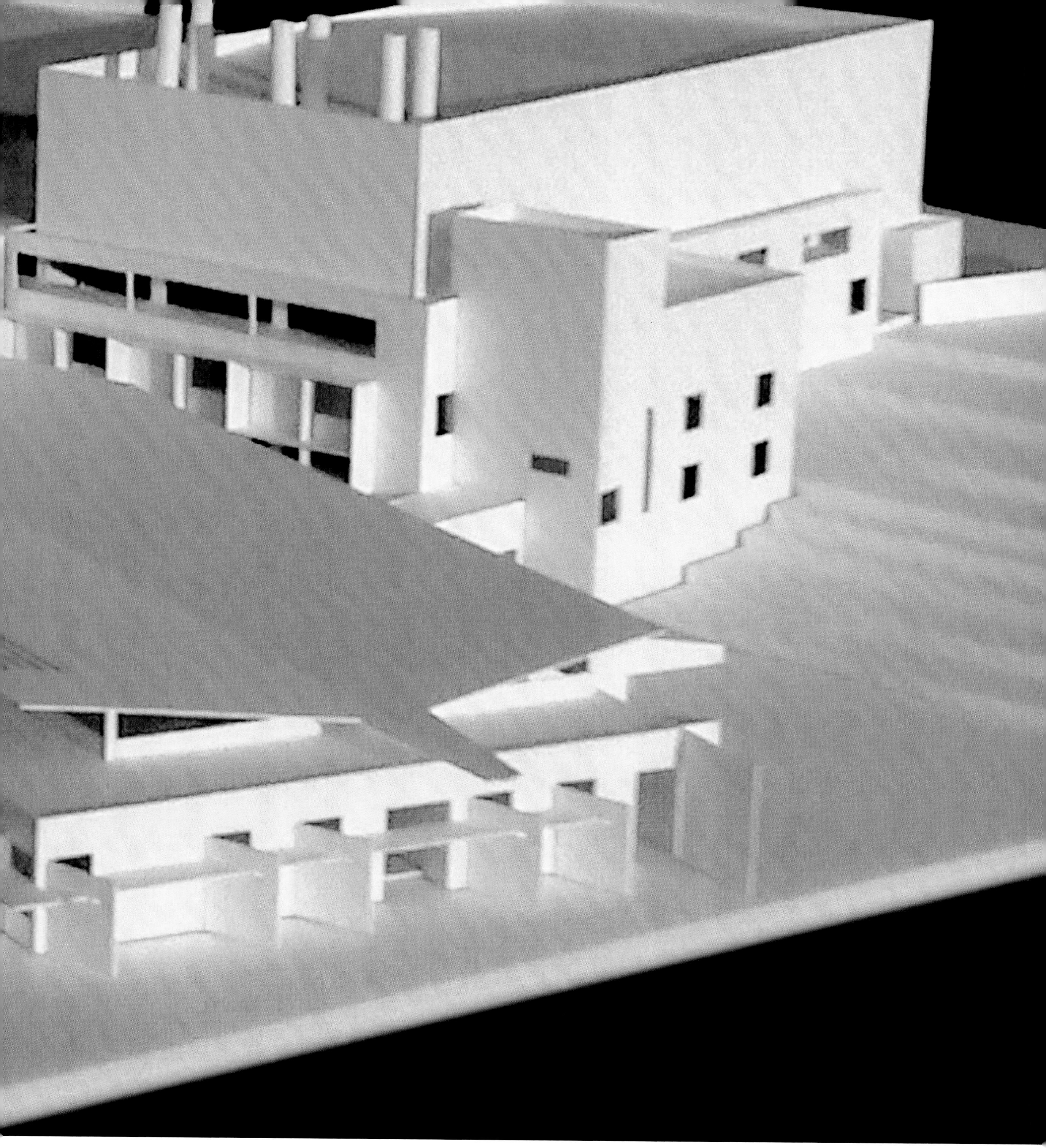

are forcing California healthcare providers to build high-quality facilities quickly in order to remain competitive. To generate the sheer number of hospitals necessary—a staggering 19 by 2013—Kaiser Permanente, California's largest HMO, needed to develop a more efficient hospital design and construction process

zation put together its Alliance Program, which partnered SmithGroup architects with contractors and owners from the beginning of the process. The resulting template hospital program has enabled Kaiser Permanente to respond quickly to the need for new facilities. Already, three hospitals in different parts of California,

several others are planned to open in successive years.

The general massing and organization of the building template was driven primarily by the functional mandates of the medical planning. The complexity of developing a project that would be

...daptable to multiple sites created ...everal challenges. SmithGroup's strategy ...as to articulate the building according ...o its internal functions and to develop ...simple vocabulary of architectural ...xpression, which would enhance the ...larity of the building and create an ...ppropriate image for Kaiser Permanente. ...s many functional elements are ...asically fixed, this expression takes ...on greater importance.

To appear more inviting to visitors and achieve a strong indoor/outdoor relationship with the landscape, the storefront building base is glazed. Above, the more private nursing units are treated in cement plaster with punched windows. Connecting the patient areas and the diagnostic and treatment block is a multi-story glass curtainwall that forms ...he primary public circulation spine and contrasts with the adjacent building elements to enhance wayfinding. A two-story glass lobby connects visitors and patients directly to the circulation spine and, with its unique circular shape, provides the central orientation node and an iconic element for Kaiser.

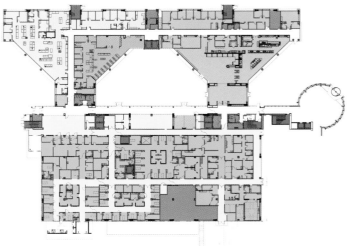

PREVIOUS: The nursing units at night ABOVE: The main entry DRAWING: Floor plan

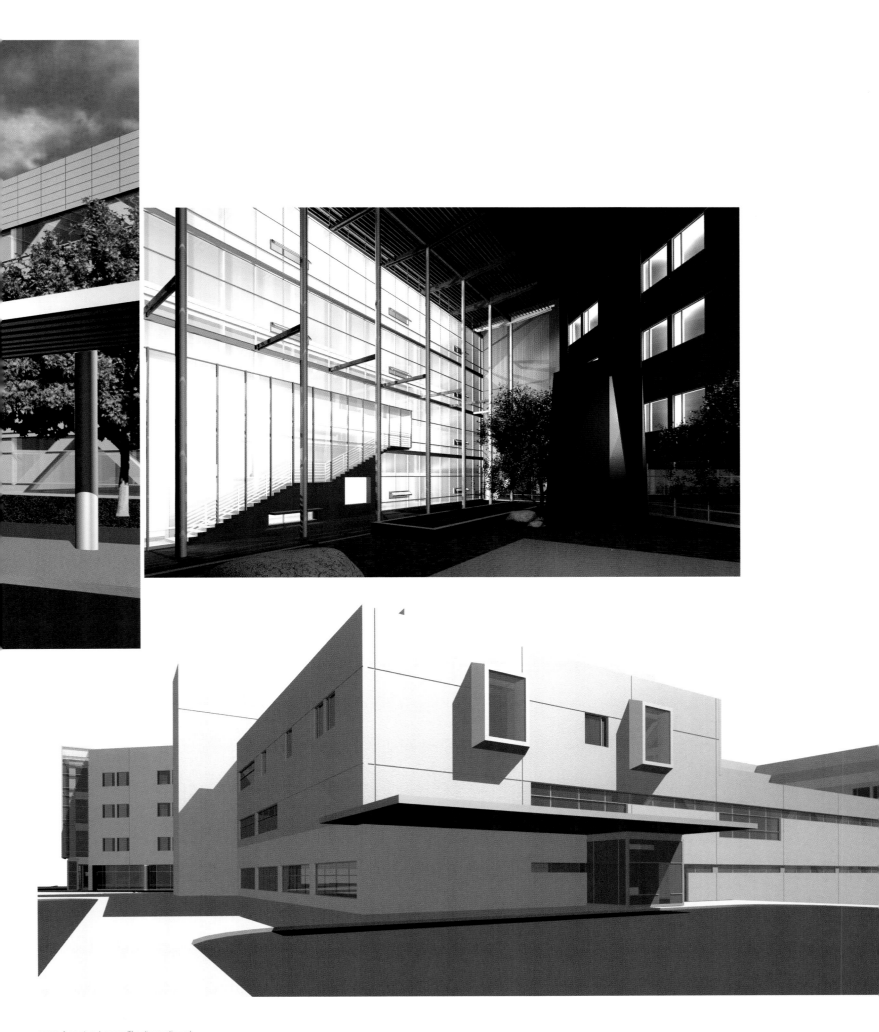

ABOVE: A courtyard BELOW: The diagnostic and
treatment wings

5

SUSTAINING THE LIFE OF A COMMUNITY

One of the quiet triumphs of postmodernism is that placemaking is a central concern for so many architects. While the aesthetics of postmodernism are out of fashion, the underlying philosophy of the movement has worked its way so far into the mainstream it is almost invisible. Even so, there remains some confusion about definitions, especially about an idea as tricky as "place". For urban projects, the typical bone thrown to those who worry about the vitality of the public realm is a few benches and planting in front of the building, and perhaps a piece of public art.

This is not an argument against open or green space in the city, rather it is a hope that, in thinking about placemaking, designers do not confuse public space with the public realm. In 1984, one of postmodernism's more sensitive practitioners, Charles Moore, tried to pin down the idea of place and how architects can make it. He defined it as "the projection of the image of a civilization on the environment. This projection can be manipulated by the architect in ways spatial and formal, but it has as its purpose not simply the making of shapes or of spaces, but the making of a sensible image of a culture, to give people a sense of where they are in it and to make the framework for whatever happens in the civilization."

Inherent in Moore's definition is a respect for specificity: it is an approach that reflects (or tries to reflect) the genius loci along with other project parameters. While his particular brand of architectural legibility has its detractors, the concern for how people will understand and inhabit a place shows a desire to enrich the common life of a given community. Moore's sensitive words could describe SmithGroup's attitude toward place as well: the firm's diverse geographical offices and practice groups are united by a firm-wide understanding of placemaking as a central element of sustainable architecture. They take a more catholic view of sustainability, thinking beyond green materials and systems (though these are certainly important as well and have been the driving force behind several projects) and understand the word to refer to buildings that give focus and clarity to their immediate surroundings. Ideally, every building would make a long-term contribution to the public realm. In simplest terms, SmithGroup architects ask themselves: will it last?

The project with the smallest footprint in this grouping actually may be the most illustrative of the firm's approach. The George Washington University (GW) in Washington, DC, asked SmithGroup to add to and renovate the Marvin Center, a Brutalist student center. The existing entrance at the ground and first floors were set back from the street and were obscured by the original split-level concrete terrace arrangement. The new lobby and entrance, a glass and metal pavilion, brings the building back out toward the sidewalk, provides a clear entry, and acts as a visual connector to other nearby GW buildings. The change is ultimately a small one, but its effects on the street and its ability to convey the attitudes of the university toward both student and city are much larger.

The contrast in scale between the Marvin Center Addition and another successful project in this category is interesting, especially as it employs preservation as a placemaking technique. Science City at Union Station in Kansas City reimagines a disused and tumbledown 1914 beaux-arts train station as the entry to a children's discovery museum, reincorporating a significant public space back into the lives of Kansas Citians. The glory days of long-distance train travel are gone, and with them, the centrality of grand stations in urban life. Spaces for children, however, are getting more and more attention and better architecture than ever before. One of the things that make Science City valuable and relevant is its deft combination of the two. The project connects visitors with a more confident period in civic architecture and unites that with an addition that, by virtue of its elegance, nods to the growing cultural tendency to value children's museum spaces. There is an implicit message of communal continuity in the pairing of the original station and its addition: even today, there is a place for grandeur in everyday life.

These two projects provide a clear and Moore-like "sensible image of the culture," and thus succeed in making or preserving a sense of place. The scales and techniques the architects employ differ dramatically, but this reinforces the idea that placemaking does not depend on the deployment of a specific technique, such as reserving some outdoor space for plantings, but a sensitivity to a building's place within the public realm.

SCIENCE CITY AT UNION STATION
KANSAS CITY, MISSOURI 1999

Designed in 1926 by Jarvis Hunt, Kansas City's famous, beaux-arts Union Station, the second largest train station in the U.S., had long been dormant. The vast hall was in shambles, and only a few Amtrak trains passed through each day. But through the collaboration of a developer, a tenant, and the Union Station Assistance Corporation the landmark building has recently undergone a transformation into Science City, a state-of-the-art interactive science museum that serves as a national model for science learning. Together with a new public plaza and inter-modal transit node, Science City restores this historic building to a central role within the culture of Kansas City.

The Science City Center comprises a 250,000-square-foot addition to the existing station structure on the site of the old rail sheds, and a faithful restoration of the great hall. In the addition, SmithGroup borrowed imagery and materials from train and industrial shed design, so that the new building is contemporary, yet evocative of Hunt's original. The saw-tooth roof recalls the old train structures that once extended over the railway tracks, and its vertical cleresto-ries use the sloped surfaces to flood the museum's "street theater" with natural light. Shade screening along the western façade guards against excessive solar heat gain, while allowing light to enter.

A glass and steel bridge with a fan canopy provides an enclosed pedestrian walkway and transparent shelter for the station's inter-modal node. The structure soars over roadways, connecting surrounding hotels, office buildings, and parks to the station's bus, commuter rail, and Amtrak rail service, further integrating the new facility into the urban fabric.

PREVIOUS: The west elevation ABOVE: The saw-tooth roof
of the exhibit shed recalls the old train structures that
used to extend over the tracks.

ABOVE: The addition as seen from the northwest
DRAWING: Site plan

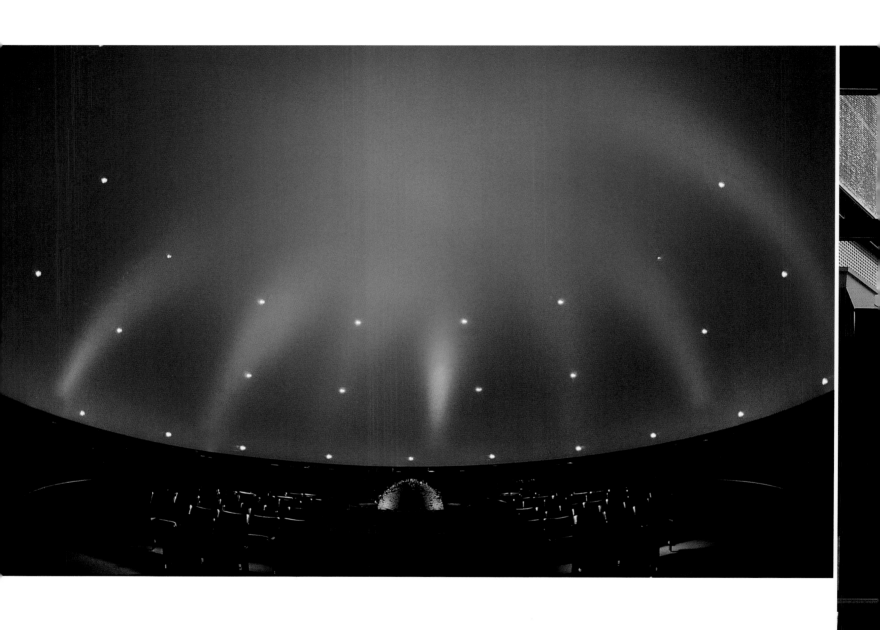

ABOVE: The planetarium

ABOVE LEFT: The north waiting room of the historic train station ABOVE RIGHT: The theater lobby BELOW: The historic station as seen from the planetarium lobby

THE GEORGE WASHINGTON UNIVERSITY
MARVIN CENTER ADDITION
WASHINGTON, DC 2002

George Washington University completely integrates into its Washington, DC, neighborhood, but for a campus, this can have drawbacks. Just as much as the university needed an expansion and renovation of its student center, it needed to add some clarity to mark the building as a gateway to the campus. The existing three-story building was packed tightly onto its urban site and left few opportunities for additions except for the terraced area at the main entrance, in which the first two floors were set back 100 feet from the street. SmithGroup's solution was to design a multi-story addition/in fill, providing 20,000 square feet of new interior space and creating a prominent new entry for the student center.

In contrast to the Brutalist architecture of concrete and split-faced concrete block of the 1967 original, the addition's exterior is enclosed in glass and metal panels and is marked by a glass reveal that separates the original building from the new. Inside, the new lobby is raised a few steps above the entry and is grand in scale, sized not only to accommodate large receptions but also to serve as a comforting pause and place of rest between the clatter of the street and the assorted functions of the building. By transforming a barren plaza into a warm, fresh, and inviting entry, the addition reestablishes the student center as the heart of campus life and serves as a catalyst for activity along a major campus avenue.

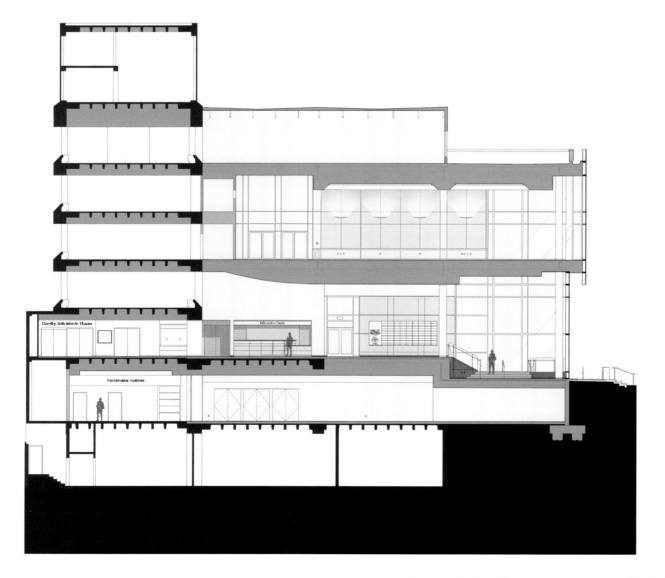

PREVIOUS: The glass façade of the addition stands out among the surrounding masonry buildings. ABOVE LEFT: The main lobby

ABOVE MIDDLE: The entry lobby ABOVE RIGHT: The multipurpose room DRAWING: Section FACING PAGE: The addition at night

UNIVERSITY OF CALIFORNIA, SAN FRANCISCO, MISSION BAY GENENTECH HALL
SAN FRANCISCO, CALIFORNIA 2002

The University of California, San Francisco (UCSF) had long outgrown its facilities on Parnassus Avenue. Neighborhood pressures prevented expansion and the steeply sloping site severely limited development options. The university decided to move its life-sciences campus to Mission Bay. Planned as a biotechnology-oriented commercial district and a large residential neighborhood, the 303-acre waterfront site, then a tangle of unused railroad tracks, industrial buildings, and empty lots, has become the city's largest development project since Golden Gate Park. The new 43-acre campus will be the focal point of a biomedical research park for private corporations. This proximity will facilitate public/private research collaboration.

Genentech Hall, which faces a green, eight-acre park, is the first campus structure to be completed. Its many functions include molecular and cellular biology, biochemistry, chemistry, structural biology, and the university's Center for Advanced Technology.

Over the last 15 years, UCSF has increased collaborative opportunities between its researchers of different disciplines in the hope of creating a more creative, innovative intellectual climate. This desire for productive collaboration became the driving force behind SmithGroup's thinking on the project, and it informed their decisions on how to organize the plan. The architects modified older design models that

separated groups of scientists in distinct laboratories. At Genentech Hall, offices have been grouped together to create collegial office suites, and the walls between individual labs have been removed to create larger sub-divisible lab spaces. At the junction point between offices and labs, there is a collective gathering/break space, which gives the lab community a focal point that both organizes the lab and allows for socialization.

The building contains many other spaces that encourage collaboration between its researchers, including a grand five-story atrium, 261-seat auditorium, lounge areas near the elevator lobbies on every floor, a café, and a 338-seat outdoor amphitheater that faces the campus green.

SUSTAINING THE LIFE OF A COMMUNITY

PREVIOUS: Daylight streams into the atrium through a skylight. ABOVE AND BELOW: Communal spaces overlook the atrium on each level. FACING PAGE: A grand stair connects each level in the atrium.

ABOVE LEFT: A multi-functional gathering space at the heart of the laboratory ABOVE RIGHT: a typical molecular biology laboratory and ghost corridor

ABOVE LEFT: The security desk in the main lobby
ABOVE RIGHT: The 261-seat auditorium BELOW: Large
windows and a raised ceiling enhance the amount
of daylight in this typical biology laboratory module.

THE MARINERS' MUSEUM
USS MONITOR CENTER (DESIGN)
NEWPORT NEWS, VIRGINIA 2003

The Mariners' Museum is a privately funded, non-profit museum dedicated to the preservation of and education about U.S. maritime and naval history. SmithGroup was hired by the museum to design the USS Monitor Center, an addition that would serve as conservation lab, exhibit space, and memorial to the world's first iron-clad warship. When it was launched in 1862, the USS Monitor changed the course of naval design, signaling the end of the wooden ship. The architects were faced with three primary challenges: how to present the size and scale of the ship in a way that wouldn't be too literal, and how and where to interpret the story of the original artifacts, which have been recovered from the wreck that still rests on the ocean's bottom.

SmithGroup created an interactive exhibit that is fully integrated into the center's design; a rough replica, or "evocation" forms a tangible impression of the ship. Visitors would thus experience the ship in its size and scale, allowing them to go "above and below the waterline," and perhaps learn what life and war was like on the Monitor. The real, recovered turret would be seen in scale, behind the evocation and separated from visitors by glass, as it goes through intensive conservation.

From the lobby, visitors would proceed down into the below grade floor of the exhibit space, seeing the evocation at eye level. The metal decking of the floor and blue-grays of the exposed steel frame are reminiscent of iron battleship construction. After experiencing the exhibit space, they would then travel through the conservation tank gallery to see the actual Monitor artifacts in conservation. From here the visitors would be directed into the museum shop.

INSET: Section

ABOVE: An evocation of the ship makes a
tangible impression.

USS MONITOR CENTER   181

SILVER SPRING TOWN SQUARE (COMPETITION)
SILVER SPRING, MARYLAND 2003

Downtown Silver Spring has been revitalized over the last decade, in part because it has great public transit access to Washington, DC, and because people rediscovered what had once been a lively community in which to live and work. The Town Square is an important piece of Silver Spring's ever-growing public realm, and will house a variety of civic functions aimed at all sectors of the community. Because of this ambitious mandate, a myriad of interests came together in its creation, including those of a developer, community leaders, a theater school, and veterans. SmithGroup accommodated all of these interests by holding a public workshop. This interactive seminar

yielded a simple diagram of the building as "porch" to the community. Building program requirements included an atrium/lobby space, great hall for meetings and performances, community program center, regional service center, Round House Theater School, administration offices, and faculty support areas. The site itself, a sliver of park that forms a pedestrian link between the residential and business district, needed to contain a veteran's plaza and pavilion for meetings, performances, and ice skating in the winter.

The 43,000-square-foot, four-story civic building constitutes the primary mass and gives form to the composition of the site. In keeping with the idea of the porch, the

square-facing façade is glazed to integrate the atrium and main circulation with the outdoor spaces. The elongated atrium, in fact, acts as a gallery, connecting the lower square to upper parking and shopping. Exhibits throughout this three-story space document the history of Silver Spring. More private spaces, including the educational facilities, community center, and theater, are on the north side of the atrium and housed in locally available stone and cast-in-place concrete. Capping the building is a garden roof, which, aside from reducing heat gain in the building and reducing storm water runoff, further integrates the building with the surrounding green space.

ABOVE: The plaza and building form a pedestrian link in Silver Spring.

TAE-JOON PARK DIGITAL LIBRARY, POHANG UNIVERSITY OF SCIENCE AND TECHNOLOGY
POHANG, KOREA 2003

One of the fastest growing and most technologically advanced universities in Korea, Pohang Institute of Science and Technology (Postech) is known as the MIT of Asia. Situated at the heart of campus, on a steep hillside, the new digital library is a computer and information center that provides a crucial hinge between the existing upper and new lower campuses. As the first building of the new campus, it sets the tone both physically and conceptually for the future of the school. Designed to be an inspiration for educational facilities throughout Korea, the library houses the latest technological advances for sharing information. Its educational center, research information center, computer center, and library components showcase the latest in IT/ Web technology, distance learning, and CAV computer systems, all of which place Postech on the cutting edge of the digital age.

SmithGroup chose to use an appropriately high-tech vocabulary, and to allow the building to express its tectonic structure with a circular five-story atrium encased in a skin of metal and glass. The transparent structure provides an open flow of universal space with high ceilings and a clear view from the ground right up through the sixth floor. Two bar-shaped buildings of stone imported from China flank the atrium, anchoring it to the earth. A grand stone stair connects the lobby with the second floor, where a sweeping monumental glass and steel staircase allows access from the second through fifth floors, connecting the upper and lower campuses with a transparent system of circulation. Visitors coming from the upper campus enter at the fifth floor, crossing a post-tension, rod supported steel bridge that spans the gap between hillside and building.

SUSTAINING THE LIFE OF A COMMUNITY

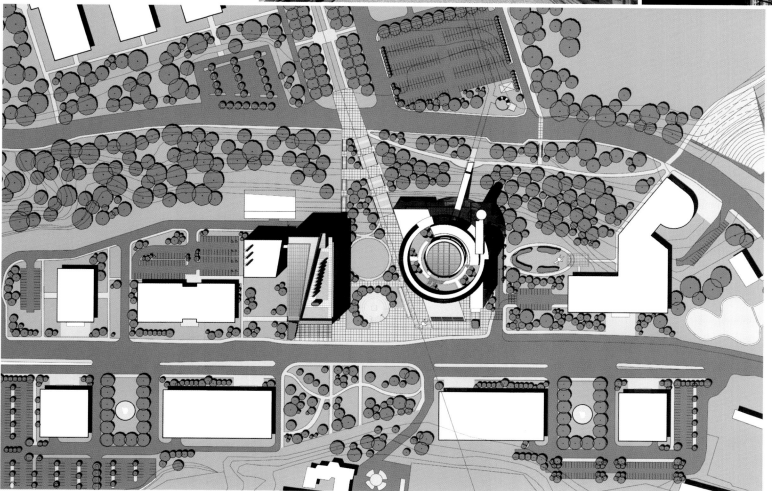

PREVIOUS: The upper-level main entrance FACING PAGE: A bridge connects the existing campus to the library.

ABOVE LEFT: A student traverses the bridge. ABOVE RIGHT: The stair enclosure at night DRAWING: Site plan

TAE-JOON PARK DIGITAL LIBRARY   187

ABOVE: A panoramic view of the lower campus
BELOW: The interior of the stair enclosure
FACING PAGE: The main entrance at night

TAE-JOON PARK DIGITAL LIB

FACING PAGE: The main lobby ABOVE: The elevators are
enclosed in glass. MIDDLE: The cyber café BELOW:
A monumental stair connects each level in the atrium.

TAE-JOON PARK DIGITAL LIBRARY   191

CAPITOL POWER PLANT
WASHINGTON, DC 2005

The Capitol Power Plant exists in an industrial zone within the Capitol area and borders on residential neighborhoods and the Southwest Freeway. SmithGroup was contracted by RMF Engineering, Inc. to develop an architectural concept design package that studies the plant's site, the potential expansion of the west refrigeration plant, and the plant's existing enclosure. The architects reviewed existing master plans and made recommendations for improvements such as landscaping, paving, and security. In addition, they developed an integrated solution to the plant's massing and exterior appearance. Power plants often face local opposition when they decide to expand, so the goal was to make the complex fit into the cityscape as a good neighbor.

SmithGroup settled on three primary strategies to help the plant better fit into the area. To soften the industrial area with plenty of green space, they proposed creating a park along South Capitol Street, planting the perimeter of the site, and extending Garfield Park across New Jersey Avenue. The effective area of the industrial zone will be reduced by reciprocally enlarging the public amenity areas surrounding it. These will include a new widened brick sidewalk at E Street and New Jersey Avenue and the removal of an administrative building berm that allows views of the historic power plant building. The overall scale of the existing buildings will also be reduced by adding new materials to provide visual variety and by terracing the South Capitol Street façade and landscape.

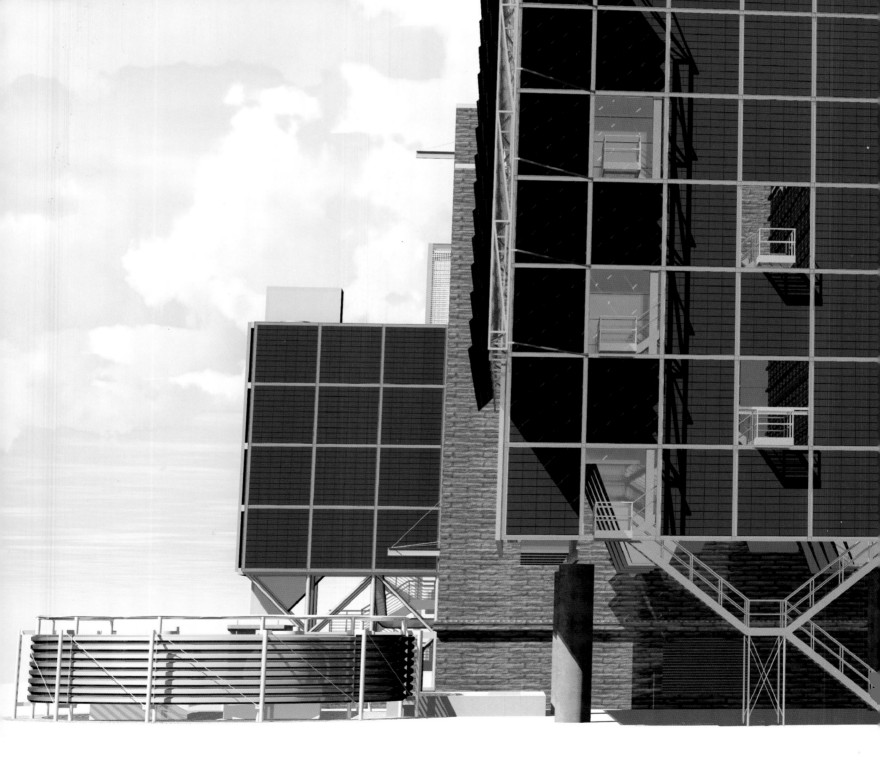

ABOVE: New materials on the existing building reduce the overall scale by adding variety.

RECENT PROJECTS

National Building Museum
Washington, DC, USA 1989

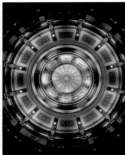

Michigan State Capitol
Lansing, MI, USA 1992

Time Life Headquarters
Alexandria, VA, USA 1997

Carnegie Institute of Washington
Washington, DC, USA 1998

Karmanos Cancer Institute,
Hudson Weber Cancer Research Center
Detroit, MI, USA 1998

Smithsonian Institution, National Museum of American History
Star Spangled Banner Conservation Laboratory
Washington, DC, USA 1998

City of Hope Oncology Clinic
West Los Angeles, CA, USA 1999

Henry Ford Museum and Greenfield
Village Menlo Park Exhibit
Dearborn, MI, USA 1999

Karmanos Cancer Institute, Alexander
J. Walt Comprehensive Breast Center
Detroit, MI, USA 1999

Shenandoah Building
Tysons Corner, VA, USA 1999

University of Southern California Newman Recital Hall
Los Angeles, CA, USA 1999

Informax
Washington, DC, USA 2000

NBCi Headquarters
San Francisco, CA, USA 2000

University of California at San Francisco
Outpatient Cancer Center
San Francisco, CA, USA 2000

Pentagon East Master Plan
Arlington, VA, USA 2001

Phelps Dodge Tower
Phoenix , AZ, USA 2001

Charles Schwab & Company Electronic Brokerage
San Francisco, CA, USA 2002

CoStar Group
Bethesda, MD, USA 2002

Fort Mackinac
Mackinac Island, MI, USA 2002

National Center for Complementary and Alternative Medicine
Bethesda, MD, USA 2002

International Spy Museum
Washington, DC, USA 2002

Takoma Small Area Plan
Washington, DC, USA 2002

201 California Street
Lobby Renovation
San Francisco, CA, USA 2003

ICF Consulting
Washington, DC, USA 2003

SmithGroup Office, Arizona Center
Phoenix, AZ, USA 2003

Terrell Place
Washington, DC, USA 2003

National Institutes of Health
Multi-Campus Facilities Master Plan
Bethesda, MD, USA 2004

Smithsonian Institution,
National Museum of American Indian
Washington, DC, USA 2004

Eisenhower Executive Office Building
Washington, DC, USA
(Phase I – 2005)

Normandy American Cemetery Visitors Center
Normandy, France 2006

Grand Hotel
Mackinac Island, MI, USA (Ongoing)

CREDITS

555 12th Street, NW
Washington, DC 1998
CONSULTANTS:
Structural Engineer:
James Madison Cutts

Mechanical/Electrical Engineer:
Girard Engineering

Historic Preservation:
Oehrlein & Associates

Lighting:
MCLA

Acoustics:
Polysonics (Phase One); Miller, Beam
& Paganelli (Phase Two)

Fire Protection Engineer:
Rolf Jensen Associates

Traffic:
Gorove Slade Associates

General Contractor:
Clark Construction Group

Client:
Manulife Real Estate

Photography:
Prakash Patel

21000 Atlantic Boulevard,
Dulles Town Center Building One
Dulles, Virginia 2002
CONSULTANTS:
Structural Engineer:
SK&A

Mechanical/Electrical Engineer:
SmithGroup

Landscape Architect:
Parker Rodriguez

General Contractor:
Tompkins Builders

Client:
Learner Enterprises

Photography:
Prakash Patel

Arizona Western
College Career Center
Yuma, Arizona 1999
CONSULTANTS:
Structural Engineer:
Landa & Associates

Civil Engineer:
Yuma Territorial Engineering

Landscape Architect:
Ten Eyck Landscape Architects

General Contractor:
Gilpin Construction Company

Client:
Arizona Western College

Photography:
Bill Timmerman

Bovard Auditorium,
University of Southern California
Los Angeles, California 2003
CONSULTANTS:
Structural Engineer:

Nabih Youssef & Associates

Mechanical/Electrical Engineer:
Mazzetti & Associates

Civil Engineer:
kpff Consulting Engineers, Inc.

Historical Consultant:
Kaplan, Chen & Kaplan

Theater:
Auerbach-Pollock-Friedlander

Acoustical:
Kirkergaard & Associates

Cost:
Davis Langdon Adamson

Lighting:
Horton Lees Brogdon Design, Inc.

General Contractor:
Clune Construction

Client:
University of Southern California

Photography:
Benny Chan

Campus Multipurpose Building,
University of California, San Diego
San Diego, California 2004
CONSULTANTS
Structural Engineer:
kpff Consulting Engineers, Inc.

Mechanical/Electrical Engineer:
IBE Consulting Engineers

Civil Engineer:
kpff Consulting Engineers, Inc.

AV/Acoustics:
Veneklasen & Associates

Cost:
Campbell-Anderson

Fire Alarm:
IBE Consulting Engineers

Landscape Architect:
Katherine Spits & Associates

Construction Manager:
ProWest PCM, Inc.

Client:
University of California, San Diego

Campus Surge Building,
University of California, Riverside
Riverside, California 2001
CONSULTANTS:
Structural Engineer:
kpff Consulting Engineers, Inc.

Mechanical/Electrical Engineer:
Henrikson Owen & Associates

Civil Engineer:
kpff Consulting Engineers, Inc.

Telecommunications:
Henrikson Owen & Associates

AV/Acoustics:
Veneklasen Associates

Cost:
Davis Langdon Adamson

Landscape Architect:
Katherine Spitz & Associates
Construction Manager:
ProWest PCM, Inc.

Client:
University of California, Riverside

Capitol Power Plant
Washington, DC 2005
CONSULTANTS:
Structural Engineer:
RMF Engineering

Mechanical/Electrical Engineer:
RMF Engineering

Landscape Architects:
Michael Vergason
Landscape Architects
Lee & Associates

Client:
Architect of the Capitol

Photography:
Tom Bonner

Chesapeake Bay Foundation
Philip Merrill Environmental Center
Annapolis, Maryland 2000
CONSULTANTS:
Structural Engineer:
Shemro Engineering, Inc.

Mechanical/Electrical Engineer:
SmithGroup

Environmental Consultant:
Karene Motivans

LEED Documentation:
Janet Harrison

Project Management:
Synthesis, Inc.

Civil Engineer:
Greenman-Pederson, Inc.

Landscape Architect:
Karene Motivans

General Contractor:
Clark Construction (GC)

Client:
Cheapeake Bay Foundation

Photography:
Prakash Patel

Discovery Communications
World Headquarters
Silver Spring, Maryland 2003
CONSULTANTS:
Structural Engineer:
KTLH Consulting Engineers

Mechanical/Electrical Engineer:
Flack + Kurtz Consulting Engineers

Civil Engineer:
VIKA Incorporated

Parking:
Walker Parking Consultants

Utility Management:
Richter & Associates

Traffic Management:
Kimley-Horn & Associates, Inc.

Geotechnical:
ECS, Ltd.

Landscape Architect:
EDAW, Inc.

General Contractor:
Clark Construction Group (CM)

Client:
Discovery Communications, Inc.

Photography:
Prakash Patel

Downtown YMCA
Detroit, Michigan 2005
CONSULTANTS:
Pool Design:
Water Technology, Inc.

Theater:
Fisher Dachs Associates, Inc.

Construction Manager:
Barton Malow Company

Client:
YMCA of Metropolitan Detroit

Estrella Mountain
Community College,
Komatke Hall
Avondale, Arizona 2003
CONSULTANTS:
Structural Engineer:
Paragon Structural Design
Incorporated

Mechanical/Electrical Engineer:
SmithGroup

Civil Engineer:
Dibble & Associates,
Consulting Engineers

Architectural Concrete Associates
Design Tec

Collaborating Artist:
Barbara Grygutis

Landscape Architects:
Ten Eyck Landscape Architects, Inc

General Contractor:
Norquay Construction, Incorporated

Client:
Estrella Mountain Community College

Owner:
Maricopa County Community College
District

Photography:
Bill Timmerman

Ford Center for Environmental &
Conservation Education, Detroit
Zoological Institute
Royal Oak, Michigan 2004

CONSULTANTS:
Theater:
Schuler & Shook, Inc.,

Experience Design:
JGA, Inc.,

General Contractor:
JM Olson Corporation

Client:
The Detroit Zoological Institute/
The Detroit Zoological Society

Freedom Fields
Lexington, Missouri 2003
CONSULTANTS:
Exhibit Design:
Gallagher & Associates

Project Economics:
Economics Research Associates

Educational Consultant:
The Learning Exchange

Developer:
Hines Interests

Landscape Architect:
Jeffrey L. Bruce & Co.

General Contractor:
J.E. Dunn Construction

Client:
National Military Education Center

The George Washington University
Marvin Center Addition
Washington, DC 2002
CONSULTANTS:
Structural Engineer:
Cagley & Associates

Mechanical/Electrical Engineer:
SME Consulting Engineers

AV/Acoustics:
Shen Milsom & Wilke

General Contractor
Whiting Turner Contracting Co. (CM)

Client:
The George Washington University

Photography:
Prakash Patel

Hangzhou Municipal Center
(Competition)
Hangzhou, China 2002
ASSOCIATE ARCHITECT:
C N A – Mr. Zhu Yijun PIC

Client:
The City of Hangzhou

Indian Springs Metropark
Environmental Education Center,
Oakland County, Michigan 2004
CONSULTANTS:
Civil Engineer:
Johnson & Anderson, Inc

Landscape Architect:
Myers Schmalenberger, Inc./Msi

General Contractor:
JM Olson Corporation

Client:
Huron-Clinton Metropolitan Authority

Indiana University School of Law,
Lawrence W. Inlow Hall
Indianapolis, Indiana 2001
ASSOCIATE ARCHITECT:
Ratio Architects

CONSULTANTS:
Structural/Civil Engineer:
Fink, Roberts and Petrie, Inc.

Mechanical/Electrical Engineer:
BSA Design

Acoustics/Telecomm:
DAOU Systems, Inc.

Geotechnical:
AC Associates, Inc.

Landscape Architects:
Michael Vergason Landscape
Architects
Ratio Architects

General Contractor:
F.A. Wilhelm Construction Company,
Inc. (GC)

Client:
Indiana University

Photography:
Timothy Hursley

Indiana University Purdue University
Indianapolis Campus Center
Indianapolis, Indiana 2006
ASSOCIATE ARCHITECT:
Ratio Architects

CONSULTANTS:
Structural/Civil Engineer:
Fink, Roberts and Petrie, Inc.

Mechanical/Electrical Engineer:
Circle Design Group

AV/Acoustics:
ideaReserve
Acoustical Design Collaborative, Ltd.
Neil Thompson Shade

Lighting Design:
Smith Group

Landscape Architect:
Ratio Architects

Client:
Indiana University

Jackson National Life
Insurance Company,
Corporate Headquarters
Lansing, Michigan 2000
CONSULTANTS:
Food Service:
Stephens-Bangs & Associates.
Incorporated

Construction Manager:
Granger Construction

Client:
William G. Vincent

Photography:
Justin Maconochie
Hedrich Blessing

Kaiser Permanente
Template Hospitals
California 2007
JOINT VENTURE ARCHITECT:
Chong Partners Architecture

ASSOCIATE ARCHITECT:
Taylor and Associates

CONSULTANTS:
Structural Engineer:
AURP, San Francisco
Mechanical/Electrical Engineer:
ARUP, San Francisco

Landscape Architect:
MPA Design

General Contractor:
HMH Builders, Inc.
The Whiting Turner Contracting
Company

Client:
Kaiser Permanente

La Kretz Hall, University of
California, Los Angeles
Los Angeles, California 2004
CONSULTANTS:
Structural Engineer:
Englekirk & Sabol Consulting
Structural Engineers, Inc.

Mechanical Engineer:
IBE Consulting Engineers

Civil Engineer:
kpff Consulting Engineers

Acoustics:
Martin Newson & Associates, LLC

Cost:
Davis Langdon Adamson

Sustainable Design:
CTG Energetics, Inc.

Curtainwall:
CDC

General Contractor:
West Coast Nielsen

Client:
University of California, Los Angeles

Lawrence Berkeley National
Laboratory Molecular Foundry
Berkeley, California 2006
CONSULTANTS:
Structural and Civil Engineer:
Rutherford & Chekene

Mechanical Engineer:
Gayner Engineers

Laboratory Consultant:
Earl Walls Associates

Landscape Architect:
Peter Walker & Partners

Code Consultant:
Cunningham Engineers

Specifications:
Douglas Day Associates

Acoustics/Vibration:
Colin Gordon & Associates

Cost Estimator:
Davis Langdon Adamson

Clean Room:
Abbie Gregg, Inc.

Construction Manager:
Rudolph & Sletten

Client:
Lawrence Berkeley National
Laboratory

MCI Center
Washington, DC 1998
PRIME ARCHITECT/
ARCHITECT OF RECORD:
Ellerbe Beckett

Mechanical/Electrical Engineer:
Girard Engineering

Civil Engineer:
Delon Hampton Associates

Chinese Architect Advisor:
John Chen Studio

Transportation:
Barton-Aschman Assoc.

Landscape Architect:
Lee & Liu Associates

General Contractor:
Clark Construction Group

Client:
Washington Sports & Entertainment
Limited Partnership

Photography:
Maxwell MacKenzie
Prakash Patel

The Mariners' Museum,
USS Monitor Center (Design)
Newport News, VA 2005
CONSULTANTS:
Structural Engineer:
Robert Silman Associates, PLLC

Mechanical/Electrical Engineer:
SmithGroup

Exhibit Design:
DMCD

Civil Engineer:
Koontz-Bryant, PC

Lighting Design:
Brandston Partnership

Client:
The Mariners' Museum

McNamara Terminal/
Northwest WorldGateway,
Detroit Metropolitan Airport
Romulus, Michigan 2002
CONSULTANTS:
Security/Communications:
Ross & Baruzzini

Acoustics:
Geiger & Hamme

Transportation Systems Engineer:
Kimley-Horn

Loading Bridges:
Ken Tuller

Water Feature:
WET Design

Signage/Wayfinding:
Monigle Associates

Food Service:
Stephens Bangs

Codes:
CCI

Passenger Tunnel Systems Integrator:
Mills James Productions

Passenger Tunnel Art Glass:
FoxFire

General Contractor:
Hunt Construction Group

Client:
Northwest Airlines, Inc.

Owner:
Wayne County Airport Authority

Photography:
Justin Maconochie
Kenn Cobb

**Motion Picture & Television Fund,
Fran & Ray Stark Assisted Living Villa
Woodland Hills, California 2006**
CONSULTANTS:
Structural Engineer:
KPFF Consulting Engineers

Mechanical Engineer:
TMAD Engineers

Civil Engineer:
KPFF Consulting Engineers

Pool Consultant:
Rowley International

Project Management:
Hutman/PM+P4D

Landscape Architect:
Land Images

General Contractor:
Matt Construction

Client:
Motion Picture & Television Fund

Phtography:
Tom Bonner
John Edward Linden

**National Academy of Sciences
Washington, DC 2002**
CONSULTANTS:
Structural Engineer:
Tadjer Cohen Edelson Associates
James Madison Cutts (Special
Structures)

Mechanical/Electrical Engineer:
SmithGroup

Historic Preservation:
Mary Oehrlein & Associates

Civil Engineer:
Delon Hampton & Associates

AV/Acoustics:
Shen Milsom & Wilke
Lighting:
MCLA

Special Artwork:
Larry Kirkland—Artist (lobby and atrium)
Don Merkt—Artist (exterior)

Landscape Architect:
Lee & Associates

General Contractor:

Centex Construction Company

Client:
The National Academies

Photography:
Prakash Patel

**National Museum of Natural History,
West Court Renovation
Washington, DC 1998**
PRIME ARCHITECT:
Hammel Green and
Abrahamson, Inc

CONSULTANTS:
Structural Engineer:
Hammel Green and
Abrahamson, Inc.

Mechanical Engineer:
Hammel Green and
Abrahamson, Inc.

Exhibit Design:
Gallagher & Associates

Food Service:
Cini Little

Theater:
W. Michael Sullivan

Construction/Cost Management:
McDevitt Street Bovis

Vertical Transportation:
Lerch Bates and Associates, Inc.

Acoustics:
Purcell + Noppe + Associates, Inc.

Geotechnical:
Schnabel Engineering Associates

General Contractor:
J.A. Jones/Tompkins Builders (GC)

Client:
Smithsonian Institution

Photography:
Maxwell MacKenzie

**National Postal Museum
Washington, DC 1993**
CONSULTANTS:
Structural Engineer:
KCE Structure Engineers

Mechanical/Electrical Engineer:
GHT Limited
Tolk (Philatelic Sales)

Historic Preservation:
Oehrlein & Associates

Exhibits:
Miles Fridberg Molinaroli

Wayfinding/Signage:
Gallagher & Associates

Acoustics:
Cerami & Associates

Security:
Sako and Associates

Life Safety:
Ferguson Engineering

Telecommunications:
Comsul, Ltd.

General Contractor:
Morganti

Client:
Smithsonian Institution

Photography:
Maxwell MacKenzie

**National Renewable Energy
Laboratory, Science &
Technology Facility
Golden, Colorado 2005**
CONSULTANTS:
Structural Engineer:
Paul Koehler Leffler

Mechanical/Electrical Engineer:
SmithGroup

Civil Engineer:
Martin & Martin

Landscape Architect:
Wenk Associates

Client:
United States Department of Energy

**P-11 Project
Xiaoshan, China 2002**
ASSOCIATE ARCHITECT:
C N A – Mr. Zhu Yijun, PIC

Client:
Wanxiang Group

**Science City at Union Station
Kansas City, Missouri 1999**
JOINT VENTURE ARCHITECT:
Ehrenkrantz & Eckstut

CONSULTANTS:
Structural Engineer:
YAS

Mechanical/Electrical Engineer:
Cosentini Associates

Exhibit Design:
Gallagher & Associates

Acoustics:
Jaffe Holden Scarbrough
Acoustics, Inc.

Noise Control, Vibration:
Cerami & Associates

Fire Protection:
Folf Jensen & Associates

Landscape Architect:
Laurie Olin

Client:
Science City at Union Station

Owner:
Hines Mortenson

Photography:
Peter Aaron
Maxwell MacKenzie

**Shanghai Municipal Electric
Power Company Headquarters
(Competition)
Pudong, Shanghai, China 2001**
ASSOCIATE ARCHITECT:
Mr. Zhu Yijun, C N A
CONSULTANTS:

Structural Engineer:
Ove Arup - LA

Mechanical/Electrical Engineer:
Ove Arup – LA

Curtainwall:
Mike Flucke and Jeremy at Benson
Industries

Landscape Architect:
Parker Rodriguez

Client:
Shanghai Municipal Electric Power
Company, Ltd.

**Silver Spring Town Square
(Competition)
Silver Spring, Maryland 2003**
CONSULTANTS:
Structural Engineer:
Tadjer-Cohen-Edelson Associates

Landscape Architect:
Sasaki Associates

Client:
PFA Silver Spring, LC

**SmithGroup Detroit
Office Relocation
Detroit, Michigan 1999**
CONSULTANTS:

Mechanical/Electrical Engineer:
SmithGroup

Lighting:
SmithGroup

General Contractor:
Crudo Construction

Client:
SmithGroup

Photography:
Justin Maconochie @ Hedrich
Blessing

**Tae-Joon Park Digital Library,
Pohang University of Science
and Technology
Pohang, Korea 2003**
ARCHITECT OF RECORD:
POS-AC.Co.Ltd.

CONSULTANTS:
Structural Engineer:
Cagley & Associates
POS-AC.Co.Ltd.

Mechanical/Electrical Engineer:
POS-AC.Co.Ltd.

Interior Design:
KDA
SmithGroup

General Contractor:
POSCO Engineering & Construction
Company, Ltd.

Landscape Architect:
POS-AC.Co.Ltd.

Client:
Pohang University of Science and
Technology

Owner:
POS - A.C. Co., Ltd.

SHAREHOLDERS

Photography:
Ki Whan Lee

**U.S. Fish and Wildlife
Service National Conservation
Training Center
Shepherdstown, West Virginia 1997**
CONSULTANTS:
Structural Engineer:
James Madison Cutts

Mechanical/Electrical Engineer:
Altieri Sebor Weibor, LLC, Consulting
Engineers

Laboratory Planning:
Earl Walls Associates

Lighting:
H.M. Brandston & Partners, Inc.

AV/Acoustics:
Acentech, Inc.

Exhibits:
Lyons/Zaremba, Inc.

Civil Engineer:
Greenhorne & O'Mara, Inc.

Landscape Architect:
Oehme van Sweden Associates, Inc.

General Contractor:
Centex Construction Company

Client:
U.S. Fish and Wildlife Service

Photography:
Prakash Patel

**U.S. Arid-Land Agricultural
Research Center
Maricopa, Arizona 2005**
CONSULTANTS:
Structural Engineer:
Paul Kohler Consulting Structural
Engineer

Mechanical/Electrical Engineer:
SmithGroup

Landscape Architect:
e group

Client:
Unites States Department
of Agriculture, Agricultural
Research Service

**U.S. Department of Energy,
Nevada Support Facility
North Las Vegas, Nevada 1997**
ASSOCIATE ARCHITECT:
Carpenter Sellers

CONSULTANTS:
Structural Engineer:
Paragon Structural Design

Mechanical/Electrical Engineer
SmithGroup

Planning:
JJR

Architectural Concrete Consultant:
Bob Kirk

Landscape Architect:
G.K. Flanagan Associates

General Contractor:
Sletten Construction

Client:
U. S. Department of Energy

Photography:
Bill Timmerman

**University of Arizona
Sarver Heart Center
Tucson, Arizona 2000**
ASSOCIATE ARCHITECT:
Dave Diebold Architect

CONSULTANTS:
Structural Engineer:
Holden, Martin, White Associates

Mechanical/Electrical Engineer:
SmithGroup

Landscape Architecture:
Wheat Scharf Associates

Civil Engineer:
Dibble Associates

General Contractor:
Lloyd Construction Company, Inc.

Client:
University of Arizona

Photography:
Bill Timmerman

**University of California,
San Francisco, Mission Bay
Genentech Hall
San Francisco, California 2002**
CONSULTANTS:
Structural Engineer:
Rutherford & Chekene

Mechanical, Electrical, and Plumbing
Engineer:
Gayner Engineers

Laboratory Consultant:
Earl Walls Associates

Exterior Design Consultant:
Zimmer Gunsel Frasca

Curtainwall:
Curtain Wall Design and Consulting

Civil Engineer:
KCA Engineering

Acoustics/Vibration:
Colin Gordon and Associates

Telecommunications:
Infrastructure Design Associates

Code Consultant:
Tim Callahan

General Contractor:
The Clark Construction Group, Inc.

Construction Manager:
Turner Construction

Client:
Regents of the University of California

Photography:
Tim Hursley
Mark Luthrimer

Abernathy, Lane R.
Anderson, Robert M.
Bagby, Barnabas P.
Ball, Maynard M.
Baur, Kevin J.
Belleau-Mills, Anne
Bhavsar, Arun N.
Billetdeaux, Neal J.
Bills, Wayne B.
Birch, Alan
Bireta, Gary
Bohn, J. Paul
Bohsali, Bassam
Brose, William
Bruce, A. Simon
Burns, Tamara
Butcavage, Thomas A.
Byma, Henry L.
Calpino, Gregg
Cardona, Victor J.
Catchot, Anthony G.
Catey, Laurie L.
Cawley, Karen A.
Christiansen, Carl
Ciupitu-Ruva, Luminita
Cobb, Kenneth M.
Colletta, Robert M.
Crain, Charles H.
Cremeans, Angela
Currie, John Michael
Davis, Harold
Denholm, Martin L.
Denison, Douglas Lee
Denny, Dennis Rockford
Diefenbach, William L.
Dimond, Constance C.
Dobbs, Michael
Dodge, Edward
Doher, Patrick M.
Elling, Roland James
Evanoff, Paul
Fekete, Bernie
Freer, Eduard J.
Frisch, Terry L.
Gazso, Barry
Gormley, John
Gott, Charles
Greenbaum, David B.
Grierson, Patricia
Guitar, Terry R.
Haley, Patricia
Hall, James
Hannon, James T.
Haraminac, David
Harriman, John
Haugen, Richard M., Jr.
Hausman, Jeffrey J.
Hebestreit, Randall
Hendrix, William H.
Henning, Ronald W.
Hopkins, Eugene C.
Hronek, David
Johnson, Paul G.
Johnston, Cynthia E.
Jones, Gregory A.
Jones, William R.
Jukuri, Mary L.
Kang, Michael
Karidis, George P.
King, David R.H.
Kirk, Michael
Kirkland, Eric L.
Klancnik, Fred A.
Kline, Andrea L.
Kline, William I.
Kosmela, Charlotte M.N.
Law, Alastair G.
Leverett, Damon
Liu, Z. Y.
Lodewyk, Mark E.
London, Joseph V.
Luckey, James L.
Machelski, Randall A.
Maher, Anthony
Manos, Theodore B.
Martino, David L.

Maves, Mark J.
McCarthy, John P.
McGunn, Michael L.
McVay, Mark
Medici, Michael L.
Mesaeh, Donald G.
Milner, Pamela T.
Mitchell, Debra
Moore, David
Mount, Michael G.E.
Mroz, Thomas L., Jr.
Murray, Barry S.
Nashed, Robert
Nolan, Michael
Nolan, Rebecca M.
O,Connell, Susan
O'Connor, Thomas F.
Ott, Steven A.
Pastore, Dominick
Patel, Kirshorchandra P.
Pearson, J. Michael
Peck, Gordon T.
Peppler, Steve
Pipas, Mark S.
Popovich, Bora
Price, Carl
Pultorak, Suzan L.
Quinn, Robert C.
Randock, Craig
Reinbold, Gerald
Richards, John
Richter, Matt
Robins, Jay S.
Roeser, Mark
Roehling, Carl D.
Rohlfing, Kenneth
Rollman, Charles Andrew
Rorvig, Timothy S.
Rose, Kirk
Rostenberg, Bill
Sass, Dale S.
Shultis, Kevin
Sienkiewicz, Gerald J.
Singhvi, Ganpat M.
Sipes, Lori D.
Simon, Esther B.
Slattery, David C.
Smith, Robert Harold
Smith, Susanne
Sobetski, John G.
Songer, Curtis A.
Stanton, Jeffrey L.
Stasa, Bart F.
Stewart, Jill
Sullivan, Kathleen
Swiech, Randal E.
Sykes, Russell P.
Thoman, Eric F.
Tobey, Philip
Tomaino, Anthony
Tonti, Paul D.
Troost, Stephen Frederick
Trusk, Joseph
Urbanek, Paul
Varner, David
Vazzano, Andrew A.
Weber, Frank J., Jr.
White, Derek J.
Wiese, Paul J.
Worthy, Gary L.
Yorke, John P.
Young, Thomas I.

AWARDS
Select Awards of the Past Decade

**America West Airlines
Corporate Headquarters
Phoenix, Arizona**
AIA, Client Award, 2002

City of Tempe, Beautification Awards, Best Art in a Private Development, 2000

U.S. Department of Energy/ Environmental Protection Agency, Energy Star Label, 2000

Southwest Contractor Magazine, Outstanding Private Building, 1999

**Arizona Western College
Career Center
Yuma, Arizona**
AIA, Arizona Chapter, Citation Award, 2001

Arizona Masonry Guild, Honor Award for Excellence in Masonry, 1999

**Carnegie Institution of Washington
Washington, DC**
Washington Building Congress, Craftsmanship Award for Lighting, 1999

Washington Building Congress, Craftsmanship Award for Restoration (Auditorium Seating), 1999

Washington Building Congress, Craftsmanship Award for Restoration (Bronze light fixtures, doors, canopy), 1999

AIA, Washington, D.C. Chapter, Award for Excellence in Historic Resources, 1999

**Chesapeake Bay Foundation,
Philip Merrill Environmental Center
Annapolis, Maryland**
NOVA Award, 2003

North East Green Building Awards/ Northeast Sustainable Energy Association, First Place, 2003

Business Week/Architectural Record Award, 2001

Building Design & Construction Magazine, Building Team Project of the Year-Grand Award, 2001

AIA, Washington, D.C. Chapter, Award of Excellence, 2001

ASHRAE-National Capital Chapter, Technology Award, 1st Place Award, Commercial New division, 2001

Washington Building Congress Craftsmanship Awards: Timber Construction, Thermal and Moisture Constructions, and Special Constructions, 2001

AIA, Committee on the Environment, Top 10 Green Building Award, 2001

**Continental Airlines
Cleveland Hopkins Airport
Concourse D, Cleveland, Ohio**
U.S. Department of Transportation, National Merit Award—Design for Transportation, 2000

AIA, Washington, D.C. Chapter, Merit

Award in Architecture, 1999

AIA, Ohio Chapter, Merit Award in Architecture, 1999

**Discovery Communications
World Headquarters
Silver Spring, Maryland**
Illumination Engineering Society of North America, Michigan Section, Illumination Design Award, 2004

Illumination Engineering Society of North America, New York Section, Richard Kelly Grant Award of Merit, 2001

**21000 Atlantic Boulevard,
Dulles Town Center Building One
Dulles, Virginia**
AIA, Virginia Society, Certificate of Merit, 2003

AIA, Virginia Society, Certificate for Excellence in Architecture, 2000

**Estrella Mountain Community
College, Komatke Hall
Avondale, Arizona**
Southwest Contractor Magazine, Best Steel Project, 2003

**555 12th Street, NW
Washington, DC**
AIA, Washington, DC Chapter, Merit Award in Architecture, 1999

Washington Building Congress, Craftsmanship Star Award for Technical Excellence, 1999

Washington Building Congress, Craftsmanship Award for Metal Fabrications, 1999

Washington Building Congress, Craftsmanship Award for Site Work, 1999

Washington Building Congress, Craftsmanship Award for Plaster and Drywall, 1999

Washington Building Congress, Craftsmanship Award for Exterior Stone, 1999

Washington Building Congress, Craftsmanship Award for Interior Stone, 1999

Washington Building Congress, Craftsmanship Award for Curtain Walls, 1999

**Ford Field
Detroit, Michigan**
Engineering Society of Detroit, Annual Construction and Design Awards, 2003

IESNA Michigan, Illuminating Design Award, Interior Lighting, 2003

IESNA Michigan, Illuminating Design Award, Exterior Lighting, 2003
da Vinci Award, 2002

**Focus: HOPE Center for
Advanced Technologies**

Detroit, Michigan
National Endowment for the Arts, Presidential Design Achievement Award, 1995

Engineering Society of Detroit, Construction & Design Award, 1995

Building Design & Construction Magazine, Modernization Award, 1994

AIA, Michigan Chapter, Honor Award, 1994

Michigan Society of Professional Engineers, Outstanding Engineering Achievement—Honorable Mention, 1994

Construction Association of Michigan, Design & Construction Showcase Award, 1994

**Fort Mackinac
Mackinac Island, Michigan**
AIA, Huron Valley Chapter, Honor Award, 2003

Masonry Construction Magazine, Historic Restoration Honor Award, 2003

Michigan Historic Preservation Network, Governor's Award, 2002

Engineering Society of Detroit, Redesign and Renovation Construction and Design Award— Historic Restoration, 2002

**Freedom Square (One),
Accenture Headquarters
Reston, Virginia**
Fairfax County - Exceptional Design Awards, Honor Award (Office), 2000

Fairfax County - Exceptional Design Awards, Honor Award (Multi-Story Car Park), 2000

AIA, Northern Virginia Chapter, Merit Award for Architecture, 2000

NAIOP, Northern Virginia Chapter, Building of the Year Award, 2000

**Freedom Square (Two)
Reston, Virginia**
Architectural Precast Association, Award for Design & Manufacturing Excellence, 2003

NAIOP, Northern Virginia Chapter, Best Speculative Office Building over 150,000 SF, 2003

Northern Virginia NAIOP, Award of Excellence - Speculative High Rise eight stories and above, 2003

**The George Washington University,
Marvin Center Addition
Washington, DC**
AIA, Washington, D.C. Chapter, Award for Excellence in Architecture, 2002

AIA, Virginia Society, Award of Merit, 2002

**Jackson National Life Insurance
Company, Corporate Headquarters,
Lansing, Michigan**

Masonry Institute of Michigan, Merit Award for Excellence in Masonry Design, 2002

Illumination Engineering Society of North America, Michigan Section, Illumination Design Award, 2001

Associated General Contractors of Michigan, Marvin M. Black, Special Recognition for Partnering Excellence, 2001

Engineering Society of Detroit, Annual Construction and Design Awards, 2001

**Indiana University School of Law,
Lawrence W. Inlow Hall
Indianapolis, Indiana**
International Interior Design Association, Bronze Award, 2002

American School & University Portfolio, Outstanding Building, Post-Secondary, 2002

Keep Indianapolis Beautiful, Monumental Award for Excellence in Design, 2001

AIA, Indianapolis Chapter, Honor Award for Excellence, 2001

**Kaiser Premanente, Sherman Way
Regional Reference Laboratory
North Hollywood, California**
AIA, San Fernando Valley Chapter, Award of Merit, 1995

AIA, California Council, Design Awards, 1995

Healthcare Facilities Management Magazine Vista Team Award, Honorable Mention, 1995

Modern Healthcare Magazine/AIA Committee on Architecture for Health, Citation Award, 1995

**Kaiser Regional Reference
Laboratory
North Hollywood, California**
Healthcare Facilities Management Magazine, Vista Team Award, Honorable Mention, 1995

AIA, San Fernando Valley Chapter, 1995

Advanced Technology Facilities Design/AIA, Review, 1995

AIA Committee on Architecture for Health,/Modern Healthcare Magazine, Citation Award, 1994

**MCI Center
Washington, DC**
AIA, Washington, D.C. Chapter, Award for Excellence in Architecture, 1998

Partners for Livable Communities, Investors in America Award, 1998
Washington Business Journal, Best Community Impact Award, 1997

**The Mariners' Museum
USS Monitor Center
Newport News, Virginia**
AIA, Virginia Society, Honor Award for Architecture, 2003

McNamara Terminal/Northwest WorldGateway,
Detroit Metropolitan Airport
Romulus, Michigan
Illuminating Engineering Society of North America International Illumination Design Award - Edwin Guth Memorial Award for Interior Lighting, Award of Distinction (tunnel), 2003

ARCHI-TECH AV Award, Institutional/Government Category (tunnel), 2003

American Council for Engineering Companies (ACEC), National Engineering Excellence Award, 2003

ACEC/Michigan Society for Professional Engineers, Engineering Excellence Award, 2003

Illuminating Engineering Society of North America Design Award, Michigan Section, (tunnel) 2003

Great Lakes Fabricators & Erectors Association, Award for Systems Excellence, 2003

Dupont Antron Design Merit Award, Public Spaces/Institutional Category, 2002

Consulting-Specifying Engineer Magazine, Project of the Year—Institutional Category, 2002

AIA, Detroit Chapter, Honor Award for Architecture, 2002

AIA, Michigan Chapter, Honor Award-Steel, 2002

Buildings Magazine, New Construction Award—Public/Government Category, 2002

American Institute of Steel Construction, National I.D.E.A.S. Award for Innovative Design and Excellence in Architecture Using Structural Steel, 2002

American Road & Transportation Builders Association (ARTBA), Globe Award, 2002

Metal Architecture Magazine/Metal Construction Association, Honorable Mention—Metal Roofing Category, 2002

Steel Joint Institute Design Awards, Unique Project Category—First Place, 2001

Michigan State Capitol
Lansing, Michigan
AIA, Honor Award for Architecture, 1996

National Trust for Historic Preservation, Preservation Honor Award, 1992

AIA, Michigan Chapter, Design Honor Award, 1992

American Consulting Engineers Council, Honor Award, 1991

Motion Picture & Television Fund,
Fran & Ray Stark Assisted Living
Villa
Woodland Hills, California
National Association of Home Builders, Best of Senior Housing

Outstanding Achievement Award, 2003

Modern Healthcare Magazine Design Awards, Honorable Mention, 2002

National Association of Home Builders, Best of Senior Housing Design Award, 2002

Nursing Homes Magazine/Long Term Care Management and SAGE, Outstanding Achievement Award, 2002

Design 2K Magazine, Long-Term Care Design Awards, Outstanding Achievement, 2002

AIA, San Fernando Valley Chapter, Merit Award, 2000

AIA, Design for Aging Review, Citation Award, 2000

AIA, San Fernando Valley Chapter, Merit Award, Master Plan, 2000

National Academy of Sciences
Washington, DC
National Design-Build Institute, Largest Category Award, 2003

Washington Building Congress, Award for Craftsmanship, 2002

National Museum of the American
Indian Cultural Resources Center
Suitland, Maryland
AIA, Northern Virginia Chapter, Award of Excellence in Architecture, 2000

AIA, Virginia Society, Award of Excellence in Architecture, 2000

National Postal Museum
Washington, DC
AIA, Honor Award for Interior Architecture, 1999

National Endowment for the Arts Presidential Design Awards, Federal Design Achievement Award, 1995

AIA, Washington Chapter, Award for Excellence in Interior Architecture, 1994

AIA, Virginia Society, Inform Award, 1994

Science City at Union Station
Kansas City, Missouri
AIA, Kansas City Chapter, Honor Award for Architecture, 2000

American Public Works Association, Public Works Project of the Year, 2000

Building Design & Construction Magazine, Reconstruction Project Award for Adaptive Reuse, 2000

SmithGroup Detroit Office
Relocation
Detroit, Michigan
AIA, Detroit Chapter, Honor Award, Renovation, 2000

Illumination Engineering Society of North America, International Illumination Design Award of Merit, 2000

Illumination Engineering Society of North America—Michigan Section, Illumination Design Award, 2000

Engineering Society of Detroit, Construction and Design Award, 2000

Tae-Joon Park Digital Library,
Pohang University of Science
and Technology
Pohang, Korea
AIA, Washington, D.C. Chapter, Merit Award for Architecture, 2003

AIA, Virginia Society, Honor Award for Architecture, 2003

University of Arizona
Sarver Heart Center,
Tucson, Arizona
Arizona Masonry Guild, Honor Award, 2002

Arizona Masonry Guild, Excellence in Masonry, 2000

Campus Surge Building,
University of California, Riverside
Riverside, California
AIA, Inland California Chapter, Merit Award, 2002

University of California,
San Francisco Mission Bay
Genentech Hall
San Francisco, California
R & D Magazine, Award for Lab of the Year—Special Mention, 2003

University of California,
San Francisco Mount Zion
Comprehensive Cancer Center
San Francisco, California
Healthcare Environment Awards, Winner, 2003

Modern Healthcare Design Awards, Honorable Mention, 2002

AIA San Francisco, Emerging Trends in Healthcare Design Exhibit, Selected for Inclusion, 2003

University of Illinois
Beckman Institute for Advanced
Science & Technology
Champaign, Illinois
Research and Development Magazine, Lab of the Year, 1990

AIA, Detroit Chapter, Merit Award, 1990

Michigan Society of Professional Engineers, Outstanding Engineering Achievement Award, 1990

AIA, Detroit Chapter, Design Award, 1990

U.S. Bureau of the Census
National Data Processing Center
Bowie, Maryland
AIA, Virginia Society, Award of Excellence in Architecture, 2000

National Endowment for the Arts, Presidential Award for Design Excellence, 2000

Federal Design Achievement Award, 2000

AIA/National Concrete Masonry, Award for Design Excellence, 1998

AIA, Washington, D.C. Chapter, Award for Design Excellence, 1998

AIA, New York State Chapter, Award for Design Excellence, 1998

AIA, New York City Chapter, Award for Design Excellence, 1998

U.S. General Services Administration, Honor Award for Architecture, 1998

U.S. Department of Energy,
Nevada Support Facility
North Las Vegas, Nevada
AIA, Arizona Chapter, Citation Award, 1999

Arizona Public Service Energy Award, 1999

NAIOP Award, Nevada Chapter, 1998

Southwest Contractor Magazine, Outstanding Public Project, 1998

Southwest Contractor Magazine, Outstanding Concrete Project, 1998

Southwest Contractor Magazine, Outstanding Architectural Design, 1998

AIA, Nevada Chapter, Honor Award, 1997

AIA, Arizona Chapter, Citation Award—Unbuilt Category, 1994

U.S. Fish and Wildlife Service
National Conservation Training
Center Shepherdstown,
West Virginia
American School & University Magazine, Gold Citation, Educational Interiors Showcase, 1998

American School & University Magazine, Gold Citation, Architectural Portfolio, 1998

AIA, Washington, D.C. Chapter, Award for Excellence in Architecture, 1997

Veterans Administration Medical
Center Replacement Hospital
Detroit, Michigan
American Society for Healthcare Engineering, VISTA Award, 1998-1999

Engineering Society of Detroit, Construction and Design Award, 1997

Michigan Masonry Institute, Michigan 'Quality Based Selection' Award, 1996

Associated Builders and Contractors, Excellence and Construction Award, 1995

ACKNOWLEDGMENTS

The work embodied in this book represents the extraordinary spirit and dedication of many, many individuals. Our talented staff, visionary clients, and expert consultants have supported us in our endeavors to be advocates for health and wellbeing, for stewardship, for the informed use of our precious natural resources, and for the exploration of the concept of "place." We live and work in a collaborative culture where ideas and knowledge are shared openly in support of the individual and project diversity expressed in this publication.

On behalf of the Board of Directors, we would like to thank all of the members of our SmithGroup team, past and present, who have helped build the legacy and shape the future of our organization. We thank our clients who shared their vision with us and allowed us to create and produce for them a unique statement of who they are. We value the expertise of our many consultants whose specialized knowledge has brought added value to each of our assignments.

To our contractors, we recognize your extraordinary efforts to meet schedules and budgets while respecting the design criteria unique to each project.

For the production of this book, we thank the marketing and graphics staff in each of our offices. They provided insight, talent, and immediate response to all of our many deadlines and requests. We are also indebted to the photographers, renderers, and model makers who have skillfully and artfully captured our projects.

We express our sincere gratitude to Dr. Bruce Alberts for his thoughtful introductory remarks. He continues to be an inspiration to everyone fortunate enough to work with him.

To Edizioni Press, we thank you for your professional guidance, creativity, and team work in shaping this book.